TECHNICAL ANALYSIS
FOR DIRECT ACCESS TRADING

THE DIRECT ACCESS TRADER SERIES

TECHNICAL ANALYSIS FOR DIRECT ACCESS TRADING

A Guide to Charts, Indicators, and Other Indispensable Market Analysis Tools

Rafael Romeu
Umar Serajuddin

McGraw-Hill
New York   Chicago   San Francisco
Lisbon   London   Madrid   Mexico City   Milan
New Delhi   San Juan   Seoul   Singapore
Sydney   Toronto

Library of Congress Cataloging-in-Publication Data

Romeu, Rafael
    Technical analysis for direct access trading : a guide to charts, indicators, and other indispensable market analysis tools / by Rafael Romeu and Umar Serajuddin.
      p.   cm.
    ISBN 0-07-136393-9
    1. Investment analysis. 2. Investments—Information services. 3. Electronic trading of securities. 4. Stock price forecasting. I. Serajuddin, Umar. II. Title.

HG4529 .R66 2001
332.63'2042—dc21

2001018695

McGraw-Hill

A Division of The McGraw·Hill Companies

1 2 3 4 5 6 7 8 9 0 AGM/AGM 0 7 6 5 4 3 2 1

0-07-136393-9

The sponsoring editor for this book was Stephen Isaacs, the editing supervisor was Ruth W. Mannino, and the production supervisor was Charles Annis.

Printed and bound by Quebecor/Martinsburg.

This publication is designed to provide accurate and authoritative information in regard to the subject matter covered. It is sold with the understanding that neither the author nor the publisher is engaged in rendering legal, accounting, or other professional service. If legal advice or other expert assistance is required, the services of a competent professional person should be sought.
—From a Declaration of Principles jointly adopted
by a Committee of the American Bar Association and a Committee of Publishers

The viewpoints and content expressed by the author are his own and not those of Tradescape.com, Inc. or any of its affiliated entities, employees, officers, directors, or authorized representatives (the "Company"). The Company does not endorse any of the content contained herein and has not verified the accuracy of any of the content. The information is not to be construed as investment advice and any reliance on the content as contained herein is at the reader's sole risk and liability.

TradescapePro™ is a trademark of Tradescape.com, Inc. and E*TRADE® is a registered trademark of E*TRADE, Inc. All other trademarked products mentioned are used in an editorial fashion only, and to the benefit of the trademark owner, with no intention of infringement of the trademark. Where such designations appear in this book, they have been printed with initial caps.

CONTENTS

PREFACE

Technical Analysis for Direct Access Trading is part of a six-book series on direct access trading from McGraw-Hill. The series of books represents the first detailed look at every element of direct access trading for individuals interested in harnessing the amazing changes occurring in the world's financial markets. All the books contain a clear and basic approach on how to take advantage of direct access to the markets for your specific level of investing/trading. Direct access trading is for everyone, and in this series of books, we show you how to take advantage of it if you only place a couple of trades a year, if you are just starting to get more active in the markets, or even if you want to be a day trader. Take advantage of these revolutionary changes today, and start accessing the markets directly with direct access trading. Good luck!

TECHNICAL ANALYSIS
FOR DIRECT ACCESS TRADING

1

INTRODUCTION

The process of investing in financial markets can be baffling and complicated, but it need not be. Indeed, sometimes friends who are not involved in the financial markets or know about investing discuss the issue in terms of complicated, ambiguous uncertainties, as if investing their savings were equivalent to stepping into some unknown abyss. Clearly, this is not the case. There is no doubt that there are plenty of unknowns in the markets, and not much can be taken for granted, but this is not the end of the story.

There are plenty of good ideas about how financial markets work, how to minimize the risks one faces when investing, and how to succeed as a small investor. Understanding the financial markets is not out of the reach of anyone willing to spend some time and effort learning about where his or her money is going. All it takes to be a good investor is the willingness to take responsibility for one's decisions and the patience to learn and understand the available alternatives. Clearly, this is not some extraordinary obstacle that the average individual is incapable of overcoming. Most people do tremendous amounts of research and learn all about breeds and breeders before buying a dog. How many of us have not read and learned about diets and health or about cars? The natural response that individuals have when making a big decision, such as what dog to buy, what car to buy, or what sort of diet they want, is to learn about the alternatives available. The same should apply for picking stocks on the market and for investment information in general.

The difference between dogs or cars and financial investing is that there is an enormous intermediary layer in financial investing that benefits directly from people not knowing too much about their investment alternatives. These financial professionals are only too willing to step in and help people with their investment decisions and take the decision-making process out of their hands. In this way, every time one of these investment professionals decides that a purchase or sale of stock needs to be made, the "cha-ching" sound of the cash register is heard as he or she nets the commissions and fees. And the best part for such professionals is that regardless of whether the decision to buy or sell is completely obtuse or not, they charge the customer the fee anyway. A broker, for example, bears none of the risk associated with the purchase or sale of stocks on behalf of his or her customers. As a result, the customer ends up putting his or her financial stake in the hands of an individual who profits from the transactions carried out on the account but not from the gains of the customer.

The alternative, of course, is for the individual to take on the responsibility of investing himself or herself. Recently, this has occurred with more frequency as people realize the potential gains sitting at their fingertips. Even the seemingly unassailable big firms on Wall Street are starting to feel the pinch. They now package themselves less as the people who should be handling one's money and more as the people who can help one handle one's money. For the first time, we are seeing big firms reach out to small investors not as if they are doing them a favor by investing their meager savings but rather by trying to somehow put together a sales pitch that will convince the customer that big Wall Street firms do offer some kind of value in their services and earn these astronomical commissions.

Even in the best-case scenario, this comes as too little too late for these big firms. They can no longer credibly pretend that their services cannot be substituted from outside the industry. The fact is that plenty of people are beginning to understand how unnecessary it is to turn to one of these big firms to invest. It is simply a question of taking the first step, and from there a person can progress to the point where he or she can invest on his or her own and understand what is going on in the markets.

In getting to this point, however, one learns and hears about different perspectives of the market. Everyone with a copy of the *Wall Street Journal* seems to have a theory as to what moves stock prices and how the markets evolve. It is not at all uncommon to hear, for example, that the more one learns about stocks in business schools, the less one knows about what really goes on in the markets. Of course, business school people usually reply that these sorts of comments are based on ignorance of the more difficult concepts and theories of markets that people who have not gone to school do not understand and that it is "sour grapes" on their part. Certainly, the idea of technical analysis as a method of picking stocks would be the sort of contentious issue about which people tend to have widely diverging views.

Technical analysis is, in short, a method of looking at stock prices, the past price history, and other market statistics relating to the stock and trying to discern where the price is heading. There are all sorts of good reasons to believe that technical analysis does not work, and there is never a shortage of individuals who articulate these arguments. On the other hand, there are all sorts of good reasons to believe that technical analysis is picking up what economists would refer to as *nonlinearities* and other features in the data that could be driven by the components of fear and greed that proponents of technical analysis argue are driving stock prices and the data. We will discuss these issues at length in this book.

The approach we take in general is to present the technical analysis as an alternative available to investors out there. If one looks to people who believe that technical analysis works, they will argue that it is gospel, and their descriptions of the effectiveness of technical indicators are usually skewed in that direction. If one looks to people who believe that technical analysis does not work, the same problem will arise. Their attitude toward technical analysis tends to skew their presentations as well. The fact is that there is no easy answer to whether technical analysis works. Recently, the National Bureau of Economic Research commissioned a paper by one of the most well-known financial economists in the United States to study the issue of whether technical indicators are any good, and he found that they contained valuable information depending on a number of factors. The approach this book takes is to plant itself squarely in the middle and completely straddle the fence. The truth probably lies somewhere in the middle, and this is where this book makes its home. There are compelling reasons to believe that technical analysis works, but this book also recommends always keeping an open mind and using plenty of common sense. This is a theory, and there are plenty of alternatives. In this sort of environment, it is good to keep an open mind.

This book is organized into eight chapters. The next chapter introduces the uses of technical analysis, with special emphasis on direct access trading and the new environment available for technical analysis as a result of this technology. Direct access trading is a combination of trading technology, Internet technology, and legislative reforms that have occurred and allowed the ordinary individual to trade from home as if he or she were on the floor of a stock exchange. This technology is similar to and evolved from the technology of the infamous day traders. It gives ordinary people the power to buy and sell stocks with the same swift execution that Wall Street firms have, but more important, it gives people the ability to see markets and information about trading activity like the Wall Street firms see. Hence they have the ability to usurp the monopoly of real-time information that was the key to Wall Street's advantages in the past. Given these advances, small investors have the opportunity to make their investments work more for them and to capture more of the surplus that results from their savings and from the risks they bear by investing in equity markets. Chapter 2 explains where the investor goes given the massive array of choices that financial markets present and where, among these choices, technical analysis can add value to the direct access trader. Note, however, that this analysis is by no means of use only to direct access traders. Quite the opposite. One of the biggest advantages that proponents of technical analysis argue that this methodology has over others is its absolute flexibility in terms of time horizon, trade size, market, issues traded, and so on. People use technical analysis to analyze all kinds of stock markets as well as other markets. We have even seen people try to use technical analysis to analyze completely nonfinancial situations. For proponents of technical analysis, this methodology is quite portable and malleable to any situation. Further topics in Chapter 2 include the basic terminology of technical analysis and a basic introduction into the rudimentary building blocks of such analysis. Having covered them, we can build on the basics in later chapters and look at the different methods used to analyze investment opportunities.

In Chapter 3 the issue of what exactly all the ballyhooing about whether technical analysis works or not is taken up with more detail. There are specific reasons why the individuals who can be loosely lumped together and called the "financial profession" argue about the validity of this methodology. One of the main reasons people in the finance profession disagree about technical analysis is that they disagree about how people think about the future. More specifically, they disagree about how other people think about the future prices of the market, what economists call *expectations*. If they cannot agree on how people form their expectations about future prices, then they cannot agree on what a good predictor of future prices is. In Chapter 3 we look at the issue of predicting prices from the perspective that future prices are a by-product of how other market participants behave, and of course, the behavior of market participants depends on prices. The chapter looks at the issue of what could be skewing the behavior of market participants and what sorts of information and timing issues are important in looking at prices. The chapter covers the efficient-market hypothesis, which, if true, renders technical analysis useless, and also looks at what sorts of questions people have about the validity of this hypothesis.

In Chapter 4 we get into the first wave of strategies for predicting price movements on equity and other markets. This chapter covers what are called *price patterns* or *price formations*. These techniques are among the most famous that are used by practitioners of technical analysis. For example, the well-known head and shoulders formation is covered in this chapter, as are many others. Building on the basics explained in Chapter 2, price charts are used to explain how these patterns present themselves and what sorts of changes technicians are expecting when they observe these patterns forming in the data. We look at the features present in price charts, whether they are some particular formation or some change in the volume that signals a change in the underlying direction of the price. Issues such as spotting sideways and upward and downward trends are discussed in this chapter, as well as the existence of primary and secondary trends. Beyond these, we discuss the different stages to which a stock price will move, whether they are accumulation or distribution periods, and patterns such as continuation and reversal patterns.

In Chapter 5 we look at the oldest and one of the most famous theories that compose the technical analysis school of thought. This is the Dow theory. It would not be unreasonable to think of the Dow theory as the "Old Testament" of technical analysis. It has been around for 100 years. When it first came out, it was not even published in a book or taught in some school; it was just a collection of editorials published in the *Wall Street Journal* by Charles H. Dow, who was one of the founders of Dow Jones & Co. The Dow theory covers some of the basic concepts on which other technical analysis ideas are predicated. It is often used to find the general direction of primary market trends. In this chapter we cover the cyclic movements of the stock market and the contribution of the Dow theory in predicting downturns in these movements.

In Chapter 6 we look at two of the most commonly used tools of technical analysis: momentum indicators and moving averages. We begin this chapter by presenting a framework for thinking about prices and how their changes come about. Based on this framework, we can identify the sources of primary price movements, i.e., the primary trend, and secondary price movements. These secondary movements bring up problems for the investor looking for buying or selling opportunities. They can lead to false signals, which are sometimes called *whipsaws*. Based on the simple price framework in this chapter, we can see where these whipsaws are showing up and what their consequences are. We then look at what taking a moving average of prices implies and how it alleviates some of the problems faced by investors. Of course, there is no free lunch, not even for proponents of technical analysis. By taking moving averages, we are alleviating some problems, but at the cost of aggravating others. We will discuss the costs and tradeoffs of moving averages in this chapter. We look at signals that practitioners of technical analysis use, particularly with respect to moving averages, such as crossovers, envelopes, and Bollinger bands. We will look at weighted moving averages and the potential tradeoff of these. Finally, we will look at the measures of momentum. *Momentum* is a generic term that covers a series of summary measures of price changes. We will look at some of these measures in this chapter and what it is that they are measuring. We will discuss the idea behind momentum and how it works in the market. We also will present a series of momentum indicators. Given the great number of such indicators, we do not present an exhaustive list, nor would we expect readers to stay focused on the ideas behind what makes momentum potentially useful if we are presenting literally dozens of different such signals. It is the view of this book that it is more important to understand the basic idea behind momentum measures and then explain some important and useful ones rather than presenting a myriad of measures, while leaving them fundamentally unexplained, and asking the reader to accept on faith that they work.

In Chapter 7 we discuss another interesting idea that occurred to a practitioner of technical analysis, who formalized it into a minor subset of technical theory. We are referring to the Elliot wave theory, which is based on the much older and more well-known mathematical idea of the Fibonacci number theory. The Elliot theory was presented by R. N. Elliot in 1939. In this chapter we examine his ideas on how things develop in a predictable series of waves and how these ideas can be used to extrapolate stock price movement information.

In Chapter 8 we present two interviews with colleagues who were kind enough to share their thoughts on the markets in general and the potential of investing with technical analysis for a small investor. One of the most important lessons in finance is that an investor facing uncertainty is usually better off spreading risk over many different assets. This is consistent with the old adage of not putting one's eggs all in one basket. One of the most important points this book makes is to keep an open mind and keep learning about how to invest. One of the best ways to learn is by listening to what others have to say, and certainly listening to others is part of keeping an open mind. Thus in this chapter we present the opinions of some of our colleagues, in the interest of presenting as diverse and balanced a perspective as possible. Of course, their opinions are their own, and we consider them to be very good advisers. However, their opinions are their own.

One final point regarding the writing of this book is in order here: This book is written in a style that attempts to be as down to earth as possible. The book is intended to be accessible to a wide range of people with differing backgrounds and levels of experience in financial markets. We do not look to back away from the more difficult or obscure concepts in the financial markets but rather try to explain them in a way that is understandable and makes the jargon of Wall Street less of a barrier for the small investor looking to become a self-sufficient investor. Our intention is to make this an accessible and understandable introductory book for people interested in technical analysis.

2

TECHNICAL
ANALYSIS BASICS

WHY ELECTRONIC DIRECT ACCESS TRADING?

Investors today have access to the markets through electronic direct access trading in a way that most market participants of decades past could not even imagine. The expansion of computer technology and the communications networks and proliferation of Internet applications have combined to produce this opportunity. Just a few years ago it would have been difficult to imagine that any individual sitting at home literally could participate in the markets in the same way as if they walked onto the floor of a major stock exchange. This is how electronic direct access trading opens up opportunities for investing.

Before the creation and expansion of computer and Internet networking technologies to the general public, the cost of market access was very high. To trade on a stock exchange, one needed representation by a physical presence in an actual exchange. That is, if you wanted to buy stocks, you needed someone to buy them for you. The number of people on the floor of each exchange was very limited in relation to the number of investors in the United States. Access to the markets for the average person came through a network of retail brokers working for large brokerage firms, which funneled the money of many investors into the market through their trading employees on Wall Street. Thus, if you wanted to buy stock, you called your broker, who sent the order in to his or her firm's trading system, where it was processed and channeled and eventually led to a trade on the exchange. This system was very expensive for small investors and everyday people because they were commanding the services and time of many professionals on Wall Street. Since small investors do not have as much money to invest, they cannot afford to spread out the cost of these professionals across a large trade, so a larger return would make it worthwhile to hire these individuals. As a result, everyday people invested very little in the market, and the market became the domain of the wealthy and larger business concerns.

As technology evolved, a combination of elements brought together what we now consider electronic direct access trading. The first was the evolution of technology that allowed individuals to participate in the markets from their computers at home. The home computer, Internet, and telecommunications technologies were combined with the evolution of electronic monitoring and order-processing systems for electronic markets. This combination opened the possibility of investing from places and individuals other than the large Wall Street firms. At the beginning, only a rare breed of individual participated in the markets using this new combination of technologies. These were the day traders. Early on, day traders mainly were people with experience in the markets, e.g., former Wall Street traders, futures traders, or other types of brokerage firm employees who ventured out on their own. As the field grew and became more regulated and stable, an environment favorable to investing for the small investor emerged. The technology of day trading has become the technology of electronic direct access to the markets, and it is allowing individuals to trade with the same tools and opportunities as the floor traders of past generations.

Today, an individual sitting in his or her home office can log on to a personal account at some dealer/broker's place of business and begin trading alongside professionals on Wall Street. The affordability of the software and trading networks that make this kind of trading possible has allowed an ever-increasing number of small investors and households to participate in the financial markets on their own. The financial firms that traditionally have filled the role of intermediary between small investors and the firms and industries that use the savings of investors are now retooling their business models to adapt to the new climate. This new climate is one where everyday individuals become more self-sufficient in terms of accessing and investing in the financial markets. Because it is no longer necessary to consult a financial professional to invest, financial professionals must make the case that they add value to the investment process of ordinary people in exchange for the fees and higher costs associated with them.

One way that these professionals may add value to the ordinary small investor is by bringing their years of experience in the markets to the investment decision. There are two parts to an investment decision: (1) what to invest in and (2) how to actually invest in it. Access to the markets through electronic means is how one can go about actually investing one's money in the markets and purchasing securities. Having the ability to do so, however, solves only half the problem. The other half lies in knowing what to do with that ability to invest directly and inexpensively. It is here that financial professionals argue they can bring something to the table for small investors. Some professionals may argue that they have a better idea of what is going on in the markets and where the money of an individual may be best suited for investing. In order to form these ideas, they use a variety of guidelines and tools of analysis.

In analyzing the current markets, professionals on Wall Street and elsewhere use many different approaches with varying levels of success. Some extremely sophisticated investors and large investment firms may use complicated mathematical models or simulations. Certainly, understanding and applying these sorts of techniques are out of reach for the average everyday small investor. This is not discouraging news, however, for the following reasons: Firms that can afford to have the absolute state-of-the-art investment professionals are not interested in, nor are they concerned about, competing with small investors. These firms are in a whole different league from everyday people. Their sheer size implies that they have to think very carefully about how they act in the financial markets. The market constrains them in ways that are very different from what small investors face. These large firms know that they can upset a price whenever they enter or leave a stock, for example, because they buy or sell so many shares. They understand that they have as one individual firm a proportionately much larger effect than any small investor. For this reason, they need to understand the markets and are willing to pay many top professionals to do the job. Additionally, they have some opportunities open to them as a result of their sheer size. By being so big, they can leverage larger investments and create different kinds of hedging opportunities for themselves that smaller investors neither have the money on the scale necessary nor the time and expertise to think up. Because the big firms have these opportunities, they exploit them. In order to do so successfully, they must hire very sophisticated investment analysts. Finally, on some occasions, the success of a large firm may come not through sophisticated investment practices but through the "brute force" exploitation of research and monitoring capabilities. These are the firms with thousands of employees watching the markets at all times, writing research reports, monitoring different indicators, and so on. These firms may not have a crystal ball to tell them the future, but what they may have is simply a way of getting information faster about what is going on. This does not mean that they can tell what will happen but that they are apprised of what is happening right away, before the general market is. In the end, all these activities need to be paid for, and the large firms must do so by generating positive returns.

For the small investor, most of these options are not currently feasible, given the level of expertise required for some of the in-depth mathematical analysis and the expense of monitoring and information services. Hence it would seem that small investors are condemned to play a secondary role in the markets and face the fact that large firms will eliminate investment opportunities of any value. If this were the case, it would seem that there is no role for small investors in the markets. There are many reasons to argue that this is not the case, however. For starters, many investors thrive on their own, by meeting their investment goals and making money on the markets every day. Also, although the investment advice of top professionals is available for large investors, it is not clear that small investors would receive the same advice if they went to a firm. If this is the case, then small investors may be better served by investing on their own than by paying high prices for second-rate investment advice. Finally, many investment professionals use alternative methods for deciding where to invest that are well within the reach of small investors. One clear example is technical analysis. Many investment professionals use technical analysis in one form or another. Small investors can do the same, reaching the same conclusions and understanding where technical analysis forecasts the stock prices and why.

In the end, the investment decisions that everyone participating in the markets makes depend on each person's own forecasts of what may happen to stock prices. Some people use technical analysis for forecasting. In this chapter we will lay out some of the basics of this as well as other methods that are employed by professional traders. Through understanding the basic jargon of the practitioners of technical analysis, we can later understand what implications arise from their methods. In doing so, we will have the answer offered by technical analysis to the question of where to invest. Thus small investors can understand the perspective of practitioners of technical analysis and any limitations of its forecasts in deciding where to invest and, furthermore, how best to use the suggestions offered by technical analysis.

THE SEA OF MONEY: WHERE ARE WE?

From a distance, the markets seem to be a jungle of investment vehicles, sophisticated market participants and traders, market instruments, and dynamic changes. While a complete description of the entire investment terrain is way beyond the scope of this book, it is useful to consider the place of small investors in this terrain to have a general idea of where they stand.

Let's consider the investment decision of a modern-day small investor. This may be someone with money set aside for future projects, retirement savings, or whatever the case may be. His or her money will flow to some investment vehicle in the myriad of available financial options. The investor may consider fixed-income instruments, which are instruments that pay a fixed amount. Stocks are not fixed-income instruments. They are variable-income instruments.

Bonds are fixed-income instruments. These are the usual investment bonds that we have all heard about, some of which are issued by the U.S. government. The federal government is by far the most well-known issuer of bonds; however, the government is not the only issuer. Corporations, state and local governments, municipalities, and other near-government organizations such as Fannie Mae issue bonds as well. As we mentioned, bonds are fixed-income securities because they pay their holders a predetermined amount. They are debt instruments used by the issuer to borrow money from the purchaser. Hence, a small investor who buys a bond is loaning money to the issuer of that bond. Usually, small investors do not analyze bond markets using technical analysis. Some investors erroneously believe that the payoffs of bonds are unvarying because the income they pay is fixed. Thus, for example, if a bond pays $100 a year, it is a fixed payment that does not vary, so the payoff has been fixed. This interpretation, however, ignores the fact that the yields associated with the changing bond prices can vary quite dramatically. In reality, bond yields and bond prices vary quite dramatically depending on things such as inflation, and there are investors who use technical analysis to look at these kinds of issues. An in-depth discussion of fixed-income investments is not of interest to us right now, however, so instead we look at variable-income investing, i.e., stocks. In the case of stocks, technical analysis is applied more commonly.

Stocks are variable-income investments because they represent ownership in companies that make varying profits from quarter to quarter. As a result, a company's earnings will vary, and so will its dividend payments. In reality, the payment made to shareholders of a company is the *dividend*, but what many investors are interested in is the company's earnings and consequently the company's stock prices. These two can vary tremendously. Note that stocks are not the only variable-income investment vehicles in the financial system. There are many others, such as commodities markets and foreign exchange markets. Furthermore, there are futures and forward markets for both foreign exchange and commodities, as well as others. A *forward market* is a market where two people make a deal but carry out the deal in the future. Thus, for example, Bob makes a deal with Sally to buy her house in 10 years, but they agree on the price today. When the 10 years have passed, Bob pays Sally the money, and Sally hands over the house. In this time, the value of the house may have changed dramatically. If Bob agreed to pay Sally $100,000 for the house and its value after 10 years is really $20,000, then Sally makes money from the deal because she sold the house for more than its current market value. If the value of the house after the 10 years is actually $150,000, then Bob makes money because he is buying the house for less than it is worth. The idea of the forward market is to fix the price of the house beforehand. These markets are useful for individuals who do not want to face the uncertainty of changing prices, e.g., a farmer. A farmer may sell a corn crop forward in order to ensure a certain annual income and not worry about the changing corn prices at harvest time. By guaranteeing his or her annual income, the farmer can plan ahead in terms of spending and eliminate much of the uncertainty. Forward contracts exist so that people such as farmers can concentrate on growing crops and not have to worry about changing financial market conditions. By selling a crop forward, the farmer can hand the risk of changing corn prices over to financial professionals who make their living by handling risks such as changing corn prices.

The futures market is very closely related to the forward market. The best way to understand the futures market is to look at the example of Bob and Sally. The value of the house may be fluctuating throughout the decade before Sally actually hands the house over to Bob. When the value of the house exceeds $100,000, Bob is making money, or is "in the money," because he has agreed to pay $100,000 for a house that is worth more than that. When the value of the house is below $100,000, Sally is in the money because she has agreed to sell a house for $100,000 even though the house is not worth as much. Suppose now that at the end of the 10 years, instead of Sally handing over the house to Bob and Bob giving Sally $100,000, the two just looked at the market value of the house and paid each other the difference. If the house is worth more than $100,000, Sally pays Bob the difference, which is what Bob would earn if he paid for the house and then resold it immediately. If the house is worth less than $100,000, then Bob would pay Sally the difference, which is what she would get if she handed over the house to Bob and then took the $100,000 and paid for another house just like it but paid less and kept the profit. Thus, at the end of the 10 years, when the forward contract expires, the difference between the price that was agreed to at the beginning of the contract and the market price at the expiration of the contract can be settled with cash. In a futures market, this difference is settled *every day*. That is, if Bob and Sally entered into a futures contract, every day they would look at the market value of the house and settle the difference between the daily market value and $100,000. The reason futures markets operate in this way is that futures contracts can be resold to anyone, and they do not have to wait 10 years to get their money, or the payoff. They get a settlement every day. By having a market for futures, forward contracts become highly liquid, and risks such as those faced by farmers can be sold to many financial market participants. Technical analysis is used in futures trading, and many traders of futures have in fact developed the methods of technical analysis over the years. While technical analysis can be used for futures, we will focus on stock markets because this is where electronic direct access traders can best exploit the present technology. In the other markets, direct access is not yet widely available for small investors, so the disadvantages of having to invest through a "middleman," or third party, can be a strong disincentive for participation by small investors.

Of the stock markets, the Nasdaq is the market of interest to us. The techniques that technical analysis gives us are certainly applicable to any of the other markets, however. We focus on the Nasdaq because it is the domain of electronic direct access traders. The reason for this is that the Nasdaq is an electronic, dealer-driven, over-the-counter market. As a result, it is a place where trading takes place solely over computers. Anyone with a trading terminal and access to Nasdaq level II data can participate in trading as if they were on the floor of an exchange. This is in sharp contrast to a centralized exchange. The New York Stock Exchange (NYSE), for example, is a centralized exchange. A small investor who wishes to buy a stock listed on the NYSE must make his or her order known in some way to a specialist, who is the person who controls trading in that stock. Thus, a small investor who wants to buy one share of General Motors must make this known in some way to the specialist who controls trading of GM stock on the floor of the NYSE. There are obviously many ways to do this, e.g., calling a stockbroker and putting in an order to buy one share of GM stock. Another way is to log on to an online broker and email an order in. The important idea here is that in order to purchase the share of GM stock, the small investor must go through an intermediary. This adds to the cost of investing because the intermediary's salary will be paid by commissions on the orders of investors. With direct access trading, this is unnecessary.

Direct access traders can trade on the Nasdaq with other investors directly, as well as with market makers in any stock that is listed on the Nasdaq exchange. There is no one individual through which every order must be funneled, and as a result, the market is spread over millions of individuals all trading with one another over their computers. These individuals can trade using traditional brokers or online brokers, but they also can trade directly with other Nasdaq market participants if they have access to Nasdaq level II data. Level II data are what give small investors direct access to the markets and a clear picture of what the various market participants are doing in relation to the purchases and sales of stock. Level II data give small investors the ability to perceive dynamic market changes and changes in the supply and demand conditions of the market as they occur. Without this information, short-run investing in the markets becomes extremely risky because small investors essentially would be blind to market conditions. By using this technology, small investors can analyze market conditions and decide what stock to buy and when to buy it.

It should be emphasized that it is certainly not necessary to have access to level II data to take advantage of the tools of technical analysis. In fact, technical analysis has existed for decades, whereas investors have not always had level II data. Investors have looked to technical analysis for guidance about when to buy and sell and what the future prices of the stocks they are buying may be. What direct access trading gives us is a clearer picture of the market for the application of technical analysis, as well as swifter and more precise processing of the purchases and sales of stock. Hence we want to focus on the tools available to small investors participating in the Nasdaq.

As mentioned earlier, the Nasdaq is structured as an over-the-counter market in which market participants trade with one another using computers or trading terminals. These terminals are linked together through the various Internet networks. Each trader uses his or her account from his or her broker/dealer to buy and sell stock on his or her computer and manage his or her portfolio. Trading occurs on special bulletin boards called *electronic communication networks* (ECNs). There are special market participants called *market makers* who trade stocks all day and are responsible for making sure that there is always someone present in the markets ready to buy and someone ready to sell. The reason for this is that the functioning of the Nasdaq depends on liquidity being present. Without it, people would be reluctant to invest in the Nasdaq because they may have trouble getting their investment dollars out. With market makers standing ready to provide liquidity, anyone purchasing Nasdaq-listed stocks knows that there is always a market participant present on the ECNs who is willing to take the opposite position on a trade. By having this liquidity present, the problem for investors is greatly simplified in that they do not have to find a buyer or seller *and* also try to find a good price. That is, investors know that any time they want (so long as the market is open), they can log on to their computer and buy or sell stock, and someone will be standing ready to take the opposite position. This is *liquidity;* any investor's asset can be converted to cash quickly at the going market price. In contrast, a real estate investment such as a house is more illiquid because it is not so easy to just sell it quickly at the going market rate. The investor must go to great lengths to find a buyer for the house and may compromise on price in order to sell it quickly. Thus investors on the Nasdaq can concentrate on finding a good price among the buyers and sellers present or just wait and transact at another time when the market rates are more favorable.

To find a good price for buying and selling, investors may consider using a trading portal such as the one pictured in Figure 2-1. Here we see the trading software called Tradescape Pro. This product is a level II data provider, and many more are available on the market (we should stress that the point here is not to advertise any one broker/dealer's software but rather to include a practical example for purposes of illustration and, more important, that our intended position is a completely neutral one in terms of which software to use or endorse). With a trading screen such as this one, any investor may keep track of the intraday movements of stocks. Notice, for example, the level II quotes, which show available buyers and sellers listed in order of best to worst prices. That is, on the buy side, the screen will show the buyers willing to pay the highest prices first, then the buyers willing to pay the next highest prices second, and so on. Similarly, on the offer side, the screen will show the sellers willing to sell for the lowest price first, then the sellers willing to sell for the second lowest price next, and so on. These software programs give investors as much flexibility and information as a professional has and allow them to participate directly. With this type of access, small investors can enter the markets better prepared and participate on a more even playing field.

Once having entered the market, small investors face the decision of what and when to buy. This is where many investors turn to technical analysis for guidance. Before clearly defining what technical analysis is and what it does, we should clearly point out what it is not and what it cannot hope to deliver. Technical analysis is *not* a "magic bullet" that will pick out the lowest price a stock will reach and tell an investor to buy and then pick out the highest price that a stock will reach and tell the investor to sell. Nothing in the world can do this—there are not many credible investment professionals who claim to know about a signal for when to buy and sell that is reliable. Technical analysis is just evidence in favor of buying or selling. It supports a buy decision or supports a sell decision, but the uncertainty of whether the decision is correct remains. We will say more about the relative merits of this evidence in the next chapter.

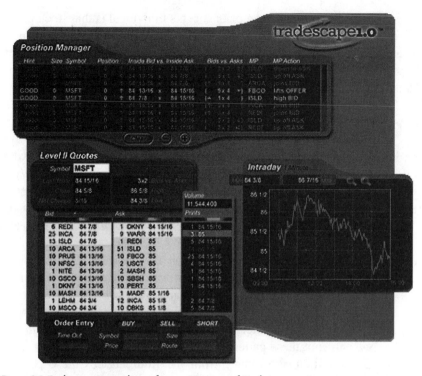

Figure 2-1 Tradescape Pro trading software. (*Courtesy of Tradescape.com.*)

Furthermore, technical analysis is more art than science. Two people using the same concepts and looking at the same data may arrive at completely different conclusions. The reason is that technical analysis contains a strong element of interpretation inherent to its application. When an investor looks to technical analysis for guidance in investing, he or she must try to be objective in evaluating the evidence presented. Because we are human, we may fall into evaluating the evidence based more on our experiences and preconceived notions about what should be happening than on what we are actually observing. In a way, we begin to see what we want to see rather than what may actually be there. Economists call the idea that a person has about what conclusions should be reached before viewing evidence a *prior*. Thus, for example, if an investor believes that the stock market falls on Fridays the 13th, then when he or she looks at the closing prices on any Friday the 13th, he or she will expect to see them falling. The prior for this individual is that stock prices fall on any Friday the 13th. Priors can be useful, but they also can be devastating if they blind an investor to evidence that could prevent losses. As technical analysis is applied, it will be crucial to try to approach every decision with an open mind and as objective an analysis as possible.

TECHNICAL ANALYSIS DEFINED

We have discussed some of the limitations of technical analysis and what it is not. Now we can turn to what technical analysis is. *Technical analysis* is the study of price movements and changes in trading volume to predict future movements of stock prices. That is, many individuals look at the history of prices and volume, and they analyze how such prices and volume behave in order to predict if prices will increase or decrease. The idea of technical analysis is predicated on the idea that prices tend to repeat their movements and changes. Thus, for example, one would argue in favor of using technical analysis insofar as the general movement of the stock market and the prices of the stocks traded therein move in ways that are discernible and predictable. As stock price movements form patterns, if we can spot these patterns, then we can take a favorable position in a stock so as to make money from the future prices these patterns predict.

Predicting the future prices of stocks has been a pastime, profession, and obsession for millions of people since organized markets began. Some theories have benefited their followers more than others. For example, there is the popular and amusing *hemline theory*. This theory says that as women's hemlines are progressively raised higher up, stock prices rise. Eventually, stock prices and hemlines both go lower. If this theory were true and panned out, it would have amusing implications for women's attire given the unusually long and uninterrupted bull market that we have seen in the 1990s. How high could hemlines go? Another interesting theory argues that whether stock prices rise or not is based on whether the football team that wins the Superbowl is from the American Football Conference or the National Football League. Another fun theory is the *greater fool or bigger idiot theory,* which states that regardless of what price one pays for a stock, a bigger fool will buy at a higher price. This one is very popular when people are trying to rationalize buying grossly overvalued stocks after entering a long bull market. Obviously, theories such as these two are stretching the credibility of serious analysis.

What we try to do with technical analysis is to look at the movements of the prices of stocks and the associated volumes and from this determine the patterns in which the market finds itself. The reason we care about these patterns is that practitioners of technical analysis believe that these patterns reveal shifts in the underlying supply and demand conditions for stocks in the markets. It is not that spotting a certain pattern in a price history reveals the future because of the pattern per se but rather that embedded in that pattern are market conditions. These market conditions are revealed to us through the patterns of stock price movements, and they are showing the transitions between excess supply and excess demand on the markets. What practitioners of technical analysis argue is that by spotting these patterns, we are spotting the changes in supply and demand that will drive price changes.

The markets are a myriad of trading and potential trading. The price at which trading occurs is an amazing phenomenon that we often take for granted but that should be highlighted because it is what we are trying to understand. At any given point in time, if the markets are functioning, we can enter the market and observe a going price for a stock. What this price represents is the lowest price that the bears are willing to sell for. When we say *bears,* we mean market participants who want to sell and believe that they should sell because prices are falling. The *market price* is the price at which one can sell; therefore, the bears in the market are selling at this price. Bears would like to sell at the highest prices possible, but they must lower their price to induce others to buy what they are selling. How low do they need to go? The answer is the market price. This same market price to which we are referring also represents the highest price at which the bulls are willing to buy. By *bulls,* we mean market participants who are trying to buy, or take the long position, because they believe that market prices generally are increasing. Bullish investors want to buy, but they would like to buy as cheaply as possible. In order to find someone to sell to them, they must raise their prices, but how high should they raise them? The answer is again the market price. Hence the market price represents the equilibrium between the two opposing forces, buyers who want to buy at the lowest price possible and sellers who want to sell at the highest price possible. This is not all, however. The market price takes on yet another role. As we have mentioned, it represents the price that keeps the current market participants happy, where bulls can buy and bears can sell. The other role that the market price plays is that everyone willing to buy or sell at this price can do so. There should be no one with access to the stock markets who cannot find a buyer if he or she is willing to sell or a seller if he or she is willing to buy. As a result, the market price serves as a buffer to all potential entrants to the markets. Every single person with stock market access is happy with the current stock price in order for the price to be an equilibrium market price. This is why it is an equilibrium price, because if it were not, it would change until no more people were entering the market or leaving, and buyers and sellers were satisfied.

What technical analysis does is look for evidence that shifts are occurring and that new buyers are entering or that current holders of a stock will be looking to unwind their positions, for example. In order to sift through the market prices for evidence of this type of market movement, practitioners of technical analysis have invented their own lingo or jargon. It is important to understand this jargon to comprehend and interpret charts. The first concept that we should understand is the basic price-volume chart.

Figure 2-2 presents a simplified price-volume chart. This is the workhorse chart of technical analysts. In fact, technical analysts are often called *chartists* for the simple reason that they base many of their predictions on analysis of charts such as the one in the figure. The top of the chart is labeled "Price," and it shows the movement of prices through time. Along the horizontal chart we would depict some unit of time, e.g., days, hours, weeks, or whatever time window is of interest to the practitioner. Along the vertical axis we would depict "Dollars" to show the changes in dollar prices. On the bottom we have the same thing, except that instead of graphing the movement of prices across time, we show the volume of trading per unit of time. For example, if this were a graph of stock XYZ based on a daily time period, then each vertical bar would show the trading volume on a given day. It is important to stress here that this chart can be based on any time period, and in fact, many different charts are used.

Notice that the price chart in Figure 2-2 shows a smooth line moving across time. For this reason, it is called a *line chart*. If it is a daily price chart, each point on the line may represent a successive price on the market on that day. Note, however, that during any given trading day, many prices occur in the markets. Only one price appears on the chart

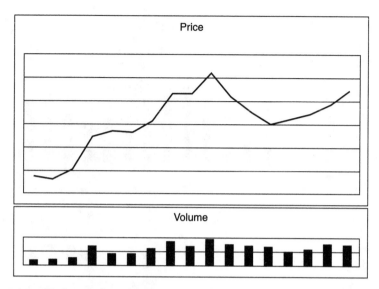

Figure 2-2 Simplified price-volume chart.

for each day; however, on that trading day there may have been a wide range of prices at which the security of interest traded. What the investor sees in the chart is only one price, perhaps the closing price or the highest price on that day. The investor has no idea about any of the other prices at which the security traded that day. This may be important information for an investor, so technical analysts use another similar chart that takes into account the trading range of the stock per unit of time. A chart that takes this information into account and summarizes it for a trader is called a *bar chart.*

Figure 2-3 shows a typical bar chart. It shows four prices that may be of interest to the practitioner of technical analysis (or technician). The first thing we want to notice is the shape of each entry in the graph. It is a rectangle with a long "tail" on top and another coming out of the bottom (in this case; in others, a tail appears only on top). The rectangles represent the opening and closing prices, and the two tails extending out from the tops and bottoms of the rectangles represent the daily high and low prices. Thus, for example, the first two entries represent days in which the lows were lower than the opening price because there is a tail extending from the bottom of the rectangles. On the rest of the days, there is no tail, so the bottom of the rectangles is the lowest point on the

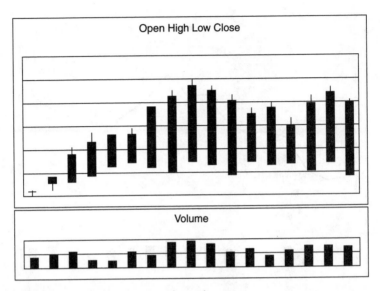

Figure 2-3 Bar chart showing trading range of a stock.

entry for these days. What this means is that on these days the opening price was the lowest price at which the security traded. Remember that the top and bottom of each rectangle represent the opening and closing prices. The fact that a day has a tail extending up from the top of the rectangle implies that on each day where this occurs, the security traded at a price higher than the closing price. Hence the stock price fell to close lower than the high each of these days. As labeled, this bar chart is called an *open high-low close chart*.

RESISTANCE AND SUPPORT LEVELS

In the preceding figures we have seen the workhorses of the practitioners of technical analysis in price and volume charts. These charts represent their eyes and ears to the world. Recall that these individuals are attempting to decipher from these charts the movements in the markets that will shift prices. In so doing they are attempting to decipher the shifts in future supply and demand dynamics themselves. That is, practitioners of technical analysis are looking to these charts to see when the market will buy and when the market will sell. One of the most basic ideas behind technical analysis is that price is being pushed by the bulls and bears and moves toward the path of least resistance. As such, it gives way to the force that is pushing the hardest, the buyers or the sellers. As buyers push harder, they will cause prices to rise. As sellers see high prices, they may be induced to sell and push prices back down. These are the two forces that move prices throughout. Practitioners of technical analysis are particularly interested in the turning points of these prices. That is, they are interested in knowing precisely the point where the price stops rising and begins to fall. This turning point is of interest to them because if they can predict it, they can profit tremendously. As such, technical analysts have noticed that for each stock, throughout the day, week, or month, there are levels at which the price for any given security bounces in the opposite direction. These price levels are the turning points for the stock price. Thus, for example, if the price is falling, it will continue to do so until it hits this particular turning point price level that we are describing here and then stop falling. At this price level, the stock tends to bottom out and begin rising again. The analogous example is that of the price rising, and then when it reaches the turning point price level, it does not continue to rise. At this point, the stock has reached its local climax and begins to fall. These turning point price levels are of particular interest to practitioners of technical analysis, and they have names. The price level at which a stock price tends to stop falling and begins to rise is called the *support*. It is also known as the *support level*.

Figure 2-4 presents a graph illustrating a support level. Clearly, the stock price moves around, but whenever it begins its falling and reaches the dotted line, the price recovers and begins to climb up again. The support is the price level represented by the dotted line. At this price, new demand sets in for this stock, and the market becomes bullish on this security. What this means is that people see that the price has fallen to this level and step in to buy it. As a result, it cannot fall lower than this level because new demand is always created. The intuition as to why this may occur is that perhaps traders see that the price always recovers at this level, so it naturally becomes a buying opportunity. Furthermore, since if the market as a whole perceives this to be the case, many people will come forward to buy the stock, and the price will increase. It will in fact be a buying opportunity. As a result, it makes sense for people to buy. Finally, if some traders do not buy on any one occurrence of this level and they see that the price increases, they will feel that they missed a buying opportunity that was evident and will wait for the price to fall again to this level. As a result, there will be latent demand for the stock that will be waiting to enter the market at precisely the support level to

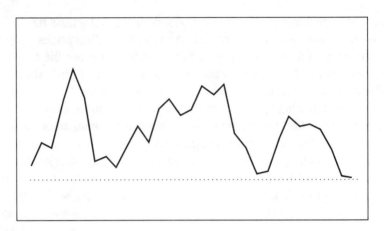

Figure 2-4 A stock support level.

get in on the next perceived buying opportunity. This will increase the demand as the stock price approaches and reaches the support level from above and will turn its movement upward.

The support level is a basic building block for many of the patterns that practitioners of technical analysis look for in the data of stock prices. As we will see in coming chapters, it is important when the price breaks through the support level, as well as when the price fails to break through the support level.

The analogy to the support level when prices are rising is called the *resistance level.* The existence of a resistance level is established when a price ascends to some price level and then falls back away from it. For example, the price will rise on the market as bullish investors push it up. In pushing the price up, the market is showing that the bulls must push harder to purchase in that they are paying a higher price, even though when one buys, one would prefer to pay low prices. Bullish investors are synonymous with optimistic investors because these individuals are willing to go higher in their bids because they feel that even though they are paying more, it is worth it. That is, the prices will continue to go higher yet. The logic behind this is that no investor would buy a stock, much less offer to pay more for the stock than it was worth earlier, if he or she did not believe that it will continue to appreciate in value. It is for this reason that we call bullish investors optimistic. And their optimism will push the stock price up so long as they need to draw in new sellers by raising the prices that they are willing to pay.

Once the price reaches its resistance level, a turn in the market will occur where the bulls no longer need to push the price higher to induce sellers to come to the market. As a matter of fact, the exact opposite occurs. Now it is sellers who need to start going lower on their prices to find someone to buy from them. They are going to lower their price until they can find enough buyers to take the stock away from them. Just as bullish investors are considered optimistic, bearish investors are considered pessimistic. The reason is that they are selling because they believe that prices will continue to fall. The logic for this is that if the prices were not going to fall, but rather rise, why would they sell? In so doing, the bearish investor forgoes the opportunity to hold onto the stock until the price rises and then sell and get a higher profit. Hence the only reason one would observe someone selling in a falling market is that the person is bearish and believes that the market will continue to fall. In such a case it makes sense to sell because if prices are falling, then it is better to sell quickly while prices are still high relative to what they will be as the market falls. Hence the resistance level is the level at which the market turns from a rising to a falling market.

Figure 2-5 presents an example of the resistance level. As prices increase toward the dotted line, they slow down and fall back away from it. For example, suppose that there are traders who hold a block of XYZ stock. Suppose also that the graph in Figure 2-5 depicts one day for stock XYZ, and some investor bought at the opening. In the market pictured here, the stock price begins by falling precipitously, right after the opening bell, when the investor had just bought. With these falling prices, the trader most likely would be interested in not selling at the low points but waiting until the stock bounces back some and then perhaps selling. Now, as the stock bounces back, the trader will perhaps sell, or perhaps will wait to see if it goes higher than the opening price, which is the price at which he or she bought the stock. Unfortunately for our trader, the price turns around and falls as it reaches its resistance level. Finally, on the second ascent, the trader may sell. Just like this trader, there may be many traders looking to unload this stock the second it hits the price at which they bought. This is called *overhanging supply*. It refers to a supply of stock that suddenly becomes available at the resistance level because there are a number of investors who bought at that price and are looking to exit the market at that price so as not to incur a loss. Unfortunately, the stock price cannot go higher than the resistance level until all the overhanging supply is exhausted, i.e., until

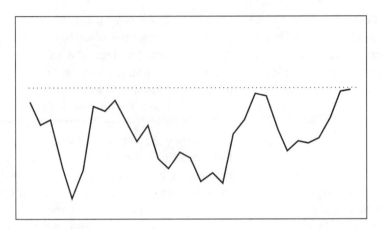

Figure 2-5 Resistance level.

all those investors anxious to exit the market at a breakeven price do so. Practitioners of technical analysis consider overhanging supply a major cause of resistance levels.

There is a very important distinction that we should note at this point that is at the heart of technical analysis. This notion is what economists call *ex-ante* and *ex-post observable phenomena.* This just means whether you can see something clearly before it has run its course completely or only after an entire process has finished. If you can see what will occur or some aspect of what will occur before the actual phenomenon, it is *ex-ante observable.* If you can only tell a phenomenon has occurred after, then it is *ex-post observable.* Usually things are only ex-post observable. This is why we have the adage that hindsight is 20/20. After something occurs, one can look back and see exactly what happened with no or relatively little uncertainty. Imagine how great it would be to be able to look forward into time and see what will happen with no or relatively little uncertainty. Then the future would be ex-ante observable. Of course, we do not have this ability, so instead we pour through charts and graphs, do calculations, and read up on what is going on in the stock markets in order to make an educated guess. The point here is that the movements of prices are uncertain. Even the best practitioner of technical analysis (or technician) is uncertain of where prices will go next. As such, even though a price has approached some resistance level in the past and turned downward, there is absolutely no guarantee that the next time it reaches the resistance level it will not break through and continue upward. As a result, what we consider a resistance level may cease to be just that as prices surge past that price level. Conversely, if we have seen prices fall a number of times in the past to some support level and then stop falling and bounce back, this does not mean that the next time prices reach the support level they will not continue to plummet further down. Ex post we can say that a price is a resistance level or support level, but we can do that only *after* we have seen the price of the stock turn and head in the opposite direction. Since this has not occurred ex ante, we cannot be sure if the price will do so when it reaches its resistance or support. The reason this is important to remember is that if this were not the case, it would be trivial to know when to buy and sell on the markets. Just buy when the stock is trading at the support price and sell when it reaches its resistance price. Of course, the people who would be selling at the support level and buying at the resistance level would be buying high and selling low. They would go broke and would be driven out of the market quickly from their losses. In fact, one always should keep in mind that whenever one looks at a chart and interprets a support or resistance level, the same chart is subject to the same interpretation by others in the market. Hence the perceived buying opportunity of one trader is necessarily the perceived selling opportunity of the trader taking the opposite side of the transaction. One of the two investors is necessarily wrong. That is, if Bob buys stock from Sally and both think they are making a wise investment, one of the two will be proven incorrect by the market due to the fact that the price will either rise or fall. Ex post we may look to the charts and see reasons and signals that agree with the correct trader, but these are not observable ex ante.

So far we have described the ascending and descending movements of stock prices. That is, we have described how bears push prices down and how bulls push prices up. The fact that we can divide the market into these two opposing forces obviously begs the question as to whether these two forces always must end up with a market that is either increasing or decreasing. The answer is that sometimes the market is neither increasing nor decreasing. In this case, the quantities supplied and demanded of the stock or of the market in general are about equal within the period of time where the market is neither increasing nor decreasing but trading is actively occurring. There are many names for this situation. In this case, we say that the market is *making a line,* and the chart shows a line. The market is called a *flat market,* a *sideways market,* or a *market trending sideways.* The market also may be called a *congestion area* because of the fact that the changes in prices are occurring in a narrow band. We can observe a sideways market in Figure 2-6.

This figure shows a flat market. Whenever the price is pushed slightly higher, it falls again back down and just keeps trading in more or less the same range. This range shows up as a congestion area and in a daily price chart is considered a horizontal movement in the price of the stock, since it traces a horizontal line across the graph. In later chapters we will see that when prices are in a flat market such as the one pictured here, the advice of technical analysts (or technicians) is to buy in whichever direction the market moves when it finally leaves the sideways trend.

When a stock price leaves the trading range of the sideways market, the stock is said to have made a *breakthrough,* or *breakout.* In this case, the stock price is pushed either higher or lower than the trading range of the sideways market. A breakthrough also can refer to a stock that is approaching a resistance level from below and continues upward. Alternatively, a breakthrough can refer to a stock price falling below the support level and continuing to descend to lower levels. As we will see in coming chapters, practitioners consider breakthroughs to be very important points of entry or exit for investors. A breakthrough past a resistance level accompanied by high volume, for example, is a sign of new higher prices for the stock. This would be a good time for taking the long position in the stock.

The general idea of technical analysis is to be able to develop a systematic set of signals that tell the technician when to buy or sell a stock. In the preceding paragraph we can see a basic example of a signal that a technician might use. In this case, high volume and a breakout would signal the direction of the market or stock price. The name for this type of signal is *technical indicator.* Such signals serve to indicate the possibility of the stock price moving in one direction or another. It is important to note here that the signals need not be based on the analysis of only one stock price; they can be used on any market index, since what performing the analysis requires is that the stock be analyzed on a graph. There are many different technical indicators, which is what we will be looking at in the coming chapters. The technician looks at a number of indicators and determines what the overall direction is for the stock, based on technical analysis. With these indicators, he or she can determine the relative strength of the technical analysis forecast of the stock price movement. If a technician sees most of the technical indicators pointing to a rising market, or a bullish market or bullish price movement,

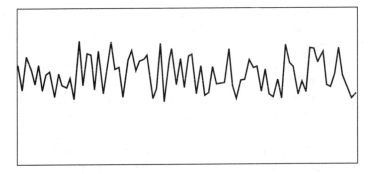

Figure 2-6 Making a line, a flat market.

the stock or market is said to be *technically strong*. If the technician sees that most of the technical indicators are suggesting that the stock price or market index should fall, then the market is called *technically weak*. Notice that there are many technical indicators; i.e., many different signals can be applied to the same situation. For this reason, technicians tend to look at a wide variety of signals and attempt to judge where the stock price is heading based on a preponderance of the evidence. Usually practitioners of technical analysis do not have one specific overwhelming piece of evidence that points them in one clear direction. Furthermore, there may be conflicting signals and unclear signals or technical indicators. If a technician is faced with conflicting and unclear signals, he or she must decide which signals to believe or whether to believe what any of them are telling him or her. Finally, the application of these indicators may depend on the individual more than on the stock price evidence itself. What this means is that the individual may bring to the table his or her priors when looking at the indicators and skew what they are telling him or her. In many cases technical analysis indicators are telling investors very little and may be of little use. Some analysts on Wall Street and elsewhere do not even believe that these kinds of indicators add any value whatsoever, as we have mentioned previously. This does not necessarily mean that technical analysis has no value for investors; there are in fact many individuals working in all areas of the financial profession who use technical analysis. It means that the technical indicators must be interpreted carefully and understood as a signal of something that may or may not occur. Technicians look at technical analysis indicators like weather forecasters look at clouds. They predict what may happen based on what they see and what their experience has taught them, but they do not pretend to know what will happen. Just as no one is sure that it will rain because clouds appear, no technical indicator is a sure sign of a change or a price swing.

When prices do change, it can be in small and slow increments. Price changes that occur in small increments during normal trading conditions show up as smooth changes on a chart. The line depicting the price movement will have no sharp upward or downward jumps because trading generally will occur at every level of prices as increases and decreases occur. Recall that charts normally show the prices at which trading is occurring throughout time. Suppose, for example, that the price of stock XYZ is 25, and then it increases to 26. Before it goes to 26, stock XYZ should be trading smoothly at every increment along the way. It should not jump from 25 to 26 all at once. Thus, for example, if stock XYZ trades at 25, we would expect that under normal conditions the stock also would trade at $25\frac{1}{16}$ for a while, as well as at $25\frac{1}{8}$, $25\frac{1}{4}$, and so on before it trades at 26. If on the price chart we see a point at 25, and the line quickly increases or just jumps to 26, this means that the market is quickly and suddenly jumping up to 26.

This type of situation is called a *gap*. A gap is a sudden and dramatic jump in the price of a stock in which no shares are traded in the intermediate price range. In the preceding example, if stock XYZ jumps from 25 to 26, then there is a gap between 25 and 26. There are many kinds of gaps, however. If, for example, the closing price of a security is 20, and the next day the security opens at 30, then the opening price is $10 higher than the previous day's close, which is called a *gap-up*. This may occur if news has been released about the stock overnight. Similarly, if the stock price at the close of the day is 20, and the next day the stock opens at 15, then the stock has *gapped down*. A gap also can occur if the lowest price at which a stock trades is lower than the highest price at which the stock trades the next day. In this case there has been a gap-down, and the price never recovers back to the previous day's low.

Some price gaps are of particular interest to technicians. Suppose that a stock price is following a general trend, be it an upward or downward trend or a flat market. In some cases, the stock may break out of the trend and gap in some direction suddenly. When this occurs, technicians call it a *breakaway gap* because it breaks away from the trend. Technicians look for these gaps to occur on high volume because it is a good indication of future movement in the stock. When a breakaway gap occurs in an upward direction on high volume, it is a bullish sign, and if it occurs in a downward direction on high volume, it is a bearish sign.

Sometimes the stock may be following a trend and suddenly gap in the opposite direction. In this case the stock may be following an upward trend, for example, and then fall suddenly on little volume. That is, the market is rising, and the stock price is increasing, and then it stops increasing and falls back with relatively little trading in the process. This type of fall is called an *exhaustion gap*. An exhaustion gap need not occur only on bull markets, it also can occur on bear markets. In this case the stock price would be falling and then would recover slightly in a gap on relatively little volume. This also would be an exhaustion gap. When this occurs, technicians believe that the price will recover and trade back to the trend and continue. That is, the gap will be filled.

An important element of a gap is that trading does not occur at some price levels. When this happens, technicians believe that the price should return to trade at the range where price levels were skipped. When a jump such as the kind we are describing here occurs and no trading is recorded at the intermediate price levels, the market has a *runaway gap*. Technicians argue that when a market shows a runaway gap, a correction will follow so that the stock can trade at the missing price levels.

In this chapter we have focused on the basics of financial analysis for technicians. We have seen the basic elements used for technical analysis and how practitioners describe market conditions. Through understanding their terminology and learning to describe stock prices and movements with the tools technicians use, we can comprehend what implications come out of technical analysis models of stock price movements. With these we can understand when technicians expect stock prices to change and how and the basis of these expectations. In the next chapter we will look at the controversial issue of technical analysis versus fundamental analysis and the question of the merit of technical analysis in the forecasting of stock prices.

3

TECHNICAL VERSUS FUNDAMENTAL ANALYSIS

THE EFFICIENT-MARKET HYPOTHESIS, FUNDAMENTAL ANALYSIS, AND TECHNICAL ANALYSIS

When making a decision to buy or sell a stock, what does an investor look at? The investor tries to act on his or her beliefs or guesses as to which direction the stock price is heading. An investor who believes that the price of the stock will increase in the future will buy; one who believes the price will decrease in the future will sell. It is as simple as this. The million-dollar question is: **How does the investor form beliefs or expectations about future prices?** *This issue is a highly contentious one, and no general consensus exists in the financial world as to its answer. Academics have spawned a whole lot of research on this topic, a lot of which is incomprehensible to the general public.*

Investors in the market are a motley bunch, and it is an impossible task to neatly divide them into categories. If we just look at the market price, we can see this. A stock's price comes about as a result of an interaction between buyers and sellers. Buyers generally buy at a specific price because they believe the price will rise in the future, and sellers sell because they believe the price will fall. Thus at any given time in the market there are people thinking exactly the opposite of others as to what will happen in the future. This chapter is about the different ways investors form expectations about the future. Everyone in the market acts on the basis of individual beliefs of how others will act. The more accurately one can predict the behavior of others in the market and act accordingly, the more successful one is as an investor.

To see how individuals in the market form expectations about the future and the importance of predicting the ways others will act in the market, let's consider an example. Suppose that the news in April is about a new mine discovered in South Africa that contains a significant deposit of diamonds. Investors also come to know that De Beers is making frantic efforts to convince the owners of the mine to limit production (so that the company can keep diamonds "reasonably priced" and also ensure for diamond cravers that "diamonds are forever"). If De Beers fails in its efforts, there will be an influx of additional diamonds in the market. It is sensible for an investor to believe that the price of diamonds will fall if there is increased supply in the market. This much anyone in the market would predict. However, there is uncertainty in the market as to whether there will be any additional supply in the market or how much the additional supply will be. The price would react based on the flow of information in the market, such as information affecting people's expectations of the outcome of the negotiations between De Beers and the mine owners. If most people are pessimistic about the outcome, then the price will fall drastically; if most are optimistic, the price will not fall by as much or will remain relatively steady. Many things can happen. Investors may overreact to the news of the mine discovery and in a panic drive down the price of diamonds. Or they may not react much because they are being patient about the outcome of the negotiations between De Beers and the mining company. Or maybe all individuals are acting rationally, taking into account all relevant information coming into the market the moment it arrives and making the price fluctuate according to all the information available. Suppose that the morning television news announces that talks between the two sides are going well. If this were the case, then price would rise. But if the late afternoon news says that talks are not going smoothly, then the price would fall.

In the preceding situation, several approaches are available to an investor. An investor who believes that other investors are overreacting should buy diamonds now while they are cheap because when the panic dies down, the price will rise again and he or she will make a tidy profit. An investor who believes that people may be unduly optimistic about the outcome of the talks or that in general investors have not reacted much to the news of the discovery of the new diamond source would be confident that price will fall. This investor would sell diamonds if he or she owns any or would sell short (that is, the investor would borrow diamonds from someone and sell them in the market only to buy them back when the price falls and then return them to the lender, making a profit in the interim). An investor, however, who believes that the market accurately reflects the price at any given moment—i.e., that investors are neither over- nor underreacting to news—should stop trying to see which way the diamond market might be heading. There is no way for the investor to predict the direction of movement. The diamond price has already adjusted to all the information there is in the market. The only way price will change is if new information reaches investors. The nature of new information is unpredictable, and as a result, one simply cannot say whether price will go up or down in the future. An investor's best shot would be to stop analyzing individual products or stocks such as the price of diamonds, and instead just buy indexed stocks, which go up or down with the market.

Whether or not one makes a profit depends on how accurately one can predict the behavior of others in the market. An investor who is wrong in his or her predictions stands to lose money. Suppose that the investor thinks that other investors are incorrect in their assessment of the market: They are overreacting to the news of the discovery of the new diamond source and are unduly pessimistic about the outcome of the talks between De Beers and the mine owners. Based on this perception, the investor would think that the price of diamonds in the market is lower than it should be and that it will rise later as the air clears. As a result, the investor would stock up on diamonds. Suppose, however, that the investor is wrong, and other investors in the market actually have not reacted enough to the news. In this case, with the passage of time the price of diamonds will fall further, and the investor will lose money because he or she bought diamonds at a higher price.

The question at hand, then, is to understand how investors act in the market. We may think that they act as superrational human beings and expect that everyone else is as rational as they are. If this were the case, they would be acting on the basis of sound information about the market. On the other hand, we may believe that investors act impulsively, getting carried away by personal hunches, rumors, and fads, creating a never-ending chaos in the marketplace. Common sense would seem to suggest that reality is a mixture of both. Humans are both rational and impulsive at the same time. Nobel Prize–winning economist Herbert Simon referred to human behavior as being "not fully rational but having bounded rationality." When economists say that people have "bounded rationality," they mean that people have only a limited capacity to keep track of what is going on around them. We can only process so much information at one time, and for this reason, we are not rational in each and every single one of our daily decisions. For some decisions we turn to others to see what they are doing so as to make our decision-making process easier. Thus we follow norms and conventions all the time without always thinking whether or not it is in our best interest to do so. This sort of behavior would explain the tendency of human beings to get caught in trends every so often. For example, how many times have we caught ourselves following the general flow of a crowd entering a stadium when we do not know where the entrance is? Or perhaps we eat too much even though we know we will not feel well later. This sort of behavior is consistent with bounded rationality in that we are not thinking through to what would be the absolute best decision, but we are pretty close. Of course, if a decision is of tremendous importance, we are likely to devote a whole lot of attention to it. Sometimes, however, this may be hard to do. In our busy world we may fail to see how important a particular decision is and thus make a quick choice before we know all the facts and then it is too late to change it. The same can hold for decisions in the stock market. We may not be able to judge the entire array of opportunities open to us in the market and follow the judgment of other investors in making our decisions.

While all market watchers and participants generally believe investor behavior to be a mixture of rationality and irrationality, they tend to differ on which one of the opposing traits dominates investor behavior and the extent to which each trait dominates the other. Some believe that although irrationality and fads do account for a part of investor behavior, at the end of the day, investors are remarkably rational. Investors thus might get carried away by a market craze and keep buying stocks of yo-yos as the price spirals upward. However, this would last only for a short while. Investors pretty soon would realize that yo-yos are, after all, not worth that much, and their price would adjust to a sensible level. Others believe that the marketplace brings together so many different minds from so many different places with access to such widely diverging information sources that on the whole the market cannot be very rational. Also, not everyone processes the same information the same way, since subjective judgments cloud the way we look at things. Thus different people would value yo-yos differently, and at the end of the day, the price of yo-yos may not represent anything particularly rational.

The point of all this discussion is that it is tied to the price movement of stocks and commodities. In trying to decide which way the price of a stock will move, a first step is to try to understand what a stock's own price reflects. Why is the price of a stock what it is, and how does a particular price come about? Investor psychology has everything to do with what information we get by looking at a particular stock quote. For example, if investors fully incorporate the information in the market, then they are using all the available information to understand what is going on around them and making educated guesses as to which way the stock price will move. In this case, the stock market can be considered *efficient*. Prices in the market adjust rapidly as new "pertinent" information related to the stock becomes available to investors. That is, investors watch TV shows and read the financial press, company press releases, and analysts' reports and use all these sources to understand and forecast changes in the value of stocks. If information flow is imperfect, or if the same information is processed differently by different individuals, then the stock price is but a reflection of all imperfections and will continue to evolve imperfectly. This means that two different people can see the same press release or the same news report on CNBC and believe that it will affect prices differently. This sort of thing happens all the time because people interpret things differently and have differing opinions on where the market is heading. If this is the case, the market can be characterized as *inefficient*. Stock prices may not adjust rapidly, and investors may not be making full use of all available information. In such a situation, prices follow trends—they rise or fall gradually, with adjustments to information taking place in stages.

How efficient are stock markets in reality? This is a question with serious practical consequences for investors. If stock prices reflect all available information in the market and adjust rapidly to new information, predicting future prices becomes extremely difficult, if not a futile endeavor. The *efficient-market hypothesis,* or EMH, argues that capital markets are indeed efficient and that future stock market prices cannot be predicted based on past and present information in the market. This is so because all available information has already been processed by market participants and is already incorporated in the stock prices. Since future information is unknown, stock prices are inherently unpredictable and follow a "random walk." The EMH was developed by academic economists and has in the past three decades given rise to many academic papers studying the efficiency levels of the stock market. The idea of the EMH has been divided into three forms with varying degrees of rigidity. That is, people believe that the stock market is just barely unpredictable, somewhat unpredictable, or extremely unpredictable depending on whether they believe in what are called *weak-form efficiency, semistrong-form efficiency,* or *strong-form efficiency.* The weak form of EMH states that one cannot predict future stock prices by looking at past stock prices. The semistrong form says that one cannot use information concerning a particular stock (in addition to simple price information) that is public knowledge to predict its future prices. Thus information available to the public such as past prices, the earnings report of a company, the state of the economy, etc. cannot help investors predict future stock prices. The strong form goes even further. It states that all information, private and public, is useless in predicting future stock prices. What this means is that even information to which only a few people are privy, such as insider information concerning new developments in a particular company, cannot help in predicting the future price movements.

The EMH thus holds stock markets to be relatively frictionless. For the EMH to work, investors must be highly intelligent and rational, and they must react immediately and accurately to all information in the market. An investor thus cannot outsmart others in the market. If there was money to be made, smart people would have made it already, so one should not dream of earning millions based on a "hot tip." Others in the market have already acted on that hot tip. The EMH view of the capital markets would be challenged if market adjustments were not instantaneous but gradual with information flow. Suppose, for example, that an underestimated company named R2D2 had developed new superfast microprocessors but that investors were taking their time to internalize this new development. The price of R2D2 stock would rise gradually as investors adjusted to the news slowly but surely. In this case, capital market efficiency would be reduced, and the market might move in predictable ways in the short run.

Directly pitted against the EMH is technical analysis. It runs counter to the weak-form EMH because believers in the weak form do not think they can look at past prices to predict future prices. According to technical analysis, past prices and trade volume *can* be used to predict future stock price movements. Proponents of technical analysis believe that the market works in cycles that are driven by factors such as mass psychology, or crowd psychology, among others. As such, the market takes on a personality and character of its own, in which rallies and declines are self-motivated at times. Investors may see others selling in the market and themselves join in selling. This, in turn, further lowers the price, and more investors see this and join in selling. The price continues a downward spiral. Investors at this point may not be thinking clearly as to what the stock might be worth. Rather, they want to limit their losses, and they engage in panic selling. An inverse scenario could lead to a buying frenzy with prices spiraling upward.

Since human actions make the stock market what it is, lots of human failings and apparently illogical and irrelevant factors may contribute to making the market move. If such factors affect stock prices, technical analysis could become a very powerful tool to analyze the stock market. The simple human failing of investors not reacting to news very fast could make technical analysis useful. Even discounting human failures, technical analysis may have a lot to offer in terms of predicting future price movements. For example, investors in the market do not have access to all relevant information simultaneously. If we believe that information filters gradually through different market investors, it follows that price would adjust continuously and gradually. The discerning investor could look at price trends to predict how the price will adjust in the future. The trick for the trader or technician (the follower of technical analysis) is to pick up a price trend (rise or fall) as it begins and to be able to foresee when the trend is about to end.

Technical analysis differs from the EMH in a couple of basic ways. Its proponents argue that not everyone has access to the same information at the same time and not everyone reacts to the same information in the same way. As a consequence, adjustments to new information are not rapid. The adjustment path can be predicted by looking at past adjustment paths, and as a result, future price movements can be determined by looking at past prices. These issues are discussed at length later in this chapter.

Fundamental analysis is another technique to look at the future potential of stocks. While technical analysis runs counter to the weak-form EMH, fundamental analysis runs counter to the semistrong-form EMH. Believers of fundamental analysis constitute a large number of highly paid Wall Street gurus and analysts who we can call "fundamentalists." They hold that every stock has an inherent value that depends on tangible factors that affect its present and future actual economic performance. Thus the inherent value of IBM stock would depend on factors such as its price-earnings ratio, its dividend payments, its levels of riskiness, the overall industry and market health, and so on. After looking at these factors, analysts can compute the inherent, or true worth, of IBM stock. If its present price is lower than this inherent value, one must buy because sooner or later others in the market will figure out its true worth; if it is higher than the inherent value, one must sell. While fundamentalists believe that future prices cannot be predicted by using past prices because past prices have nothing to do with a stock's true worth, they do believe that future prices can be predicted if broader indicators are looked at.

In the remainder of this chapter we will discuss the EMH and its three forms. We will see what evidence there is for and against the EMH. We will discuss the strengths and weaknesses of fundamental analysis and technical analysis at greater length. This will enable you to get a clearer idea as to the different ways scholars and investors view the nature of the capital market.

THE EFFICIENT-MARKET HYPOTHESIS

Expectations of the future play a crucial role in all our economic decisions. If we expect our income to be lower in the future, we will reduce our consumption today and save up for the future. If a company like Dell expects the economy to continue booming for another year, it will anticipate higher sales of its product and hire additional workers. Especially in the financial market, expectations play a major role as to how investors act. If people expect the Federal Reserve to raise interest rates in its next open committee meeting because it feels the economy is overheating and needs to be reigned in, stock prices will fall as economic growth prospects slow down.

In the 1950s and 1960s, the prevalent view among economists was that expectations about the future depended to a large extent on the past. Individuals looked at past history and upgraded their expectations of the future based on that. This way of forming expectations based on the past is called *adaptive expectations*. Thus, if in the United States inflation has been rising at a 3 percent yearly rate, expectations about future inflation will be roughly 3 percent. If inflation were to jump suddenly to 6 percent, expectations about future inflation would not rise to 6 percent at once because people are used to 3 percent inflation. It would rise to 6 percent only gradually. This way of expectation formation seemed a bit unsatisfactory to economists. It meant that individuals look only at the past history of one variable to predict its future value, whereas other factors might be affecting its future value. Expectations of inflation probably should include such factors as money supply increase or the interest rate the Fed sets, not merely what past inflation was previously.

An alternative explanation of expectations that came to dominate economics was that of *rational expectations*. Under rational expectations, individuals are seen to make their predictions of the future based on all the information they have, and the expectations thus formed are the best or most efficient forecasts of the future. This means that one's best guess about the future will be based on all the information one has now. Thus expectations of future inflation would not be based merely on past inflation history; rather, they would be based on more fundamental features of the economy such as the money supply growth, interest rates, and so on. Even under rational expectations, individuals may well be wrong in their predictions of the future. An individual's estimation of inflation may be 6 percent, whereas in reality it might turn out to be 6.2 percent. This could result from not having all the information pertinent to the future available at hand. Regardless, as long as expectations are formed taking into account all *available* information, they are considered rational.

The rational expectations theory was incorporated into financial economics, and this is what led to development of the EMH. In the financial markets, the incentives to make efficient forecasts about the future are particularly strong given the huge amount of money individuals stand to gain by making accurate predictions. Suppose that the price of IBM stock today is $100. An investor researches the company and the market conditions and predicts that the price of IBM stock 3 months from now will rise to $120. An investor who is correct in this prediction stands to gain

$20 per stock by buying the stock now. On the other hand, suppose that a sloppy investor ignores market conditions and predicts that IBM price actually will fall to $90 in 3 months. He or she thus would sell IBM stock now for $100 and lose out on the huge profit opportunity. The EMH argues that when the penalties of inefficiency (meaning the costs of not taking into account all relevant information) are so high, few individuals could continue to remain inefficient and last in the market. Individuals in the market in general would be efficient about their predictions of the future. Consequently, the stock market would be efficient. What *efficiency* here implies is that obvious profit opportunities from forecasting future prices would diminish. Let's see how. Since all rational investors would bring into account all relevant information while thinking about the future, they would realize that the price of IBM stock in the future would be $120. They would all rush to buy IBM stock now and sell high later. Since investors would rush in to buy, they would drive its price up very fast, and before we know it, IBM stock would be trading at $120, and any one investor's hope of making millions by buying IBM low and selling high would evaporate. This is what economists mean when they say that a market is efficient. Others out there are as smart as you or even smarter than you, and everyone is trying to outsmart each other. However, no one succeeds because every profit-maximizing investor is thinking roughly the same way and catching on to what others are doing very quickly.

The rational expectations of investors make the stock market efficient. Investors follow the market closely and internalize new information swiftly. As a result, information that is public cannot help one predict future prices because stock prices have already adjusted to it. Information on IBM that was available to investors led its price to jump to $120 almost immediately. All one can say with certainty is what the present holds, not what will happen in 3 months.

We already mentioned the three forms of the EMH: weak, semistrong, and strong. The weak form states that past stock prices cannot predict future stock prices. Since all prices are fully adjusted based on the information already available in the market, how can one possibly predict correctly the direction in which price will move unless new information has become available to the market? If we know that the price of IBM stock is $110 today, was $100 yesterday, and was $95 the day before, we cannot predict what its price will be tomorrow based on this price information only. Its price tomorrow can be anything. However, a believer in technical analysis may think that the IBM stock is showing a rising trend and therefore that its price will be higher than \$110 tomorrow. Technical analysis, which is based on prices moving in trends and thus being predictable, is anathema to the weak-form EMH.

The semistrong-form EMH encompasses the weak form and goes a step further. Not only are past prices useless in predicting future movements of a stock, a careful consideration of past data of a firm's overall financial and economic health is equally useless in predicting future price movements. This is bad news for the Wall Street firms that conduct extensive industry and market analysis, i.e., fundamental analysis, to project future movements in stocks. The semistrong form holds that such analysis is not of value because it is based on public information about the market and particular stocks. Any public information already would be reflected in stock prices. Only information to which a select few are privy, say, insider information about a particular company, can give one an edge in predicting the future of a stock price. However, this is about it. According to the semistrong form, the ordinary investor simply should throw in the towel. He or she has no chance of beating the market. Even if the investor were to get advice from analysts on Wall Street, he or she could not better the market returns because everyone else would have the same information and act on it. It is not that the advice of stock analysts is absolutely useless, but the advice costs money (since it also costs analysts to gather information), and once these costs are brought into account, one cannot beat the market. Suppose that an investment adviser forecasts to clients that the price of IBM stock will rise from \$100 today to be around \$120 one month from now and advises that they buy IBM stock today and sell a month later. If the advice were accurate and free of charge, clients would make a \$20 profit per stock. However, for this piece of information, the investment adviser will charge clients a fee, and after this fee is brought into account, a client's gain may very well be insignificant from trading based on the information about IBM's price rise. Of course, an interesting question is: Why do Wall Street analysts exist and thrive year after year if they add no value to investors?

The strong-form EMH suggests a stronger form of market efficiency than either the weak or the semistrong form. Under the strong form, no information, public or private, can help one predict future movements in stock prices. There is no way for a group of investors to have access to valuable information (not available to the general public) that would enable them to make superlarge profits. Even insider information is useless because it is very difficult for insiders to act on such information without others in the market catching on. Not only does the strong form assume efficient markets, it also assumes perfect markets. By *perfect markets,* economists mean a market in which information is free of cost and available to all. The strong form would suggest something even more startling to the common investor: The market is so efficient that one investment is as good as another. Individuals have made use of all the information in the market and have bought and sold securities to the point where they have equated the expected returns from all of them. After all, why would an investor continue to hold onto a particular stock if he or she knows that by switching to another he or she can be a fraction better off? Thus the strong-form EMH implies that it does not matter whether one holds Microsoft stocks or Frito Lay stocks.

All this discussion has been at an intuitive level. What is the real-world evidence on EMH? What does the endurance of technicians, investment analysts, and advisers tell us about EMH? Let's now turn to evidence for and against the EMH.

EVIDENCE ON EMH

Early evidence on the EMH was strong, and a considerable amount of academic research seemed to corroborate it. Subsequent analysis has cast into doubt some of its suggestions. A famous economist by the name of Eugene Fama, who formalized the EMH through his path-breaking work, made initial attempts to synthesize the different evidence on the EMH. Since then, many have followed and made a living in academia studying evidence on the EMH.

A test of the weak-form EMH is to see whether price movements are independent of previous price movements. Several studies actually have found no evidence of stock prices being systematically correlated from one period to another. If this were true, for example, one would not be able to look at a downward price movement over the past 10 days to predict that prices also would fall on the eleventh day. Surely a stock's price may move in the same direction for a few straight periods, but this is not evidence of correlation. The way to test for correlation is to formulate how a stock price would fluctuate in a random process and then compare that with actual market price fluctuations. If there is no statistical difference between the two, we can conclude that the stock market does not follow any predictable patterns.

The weak-form EMH would argue that since future prices cannot be predicted from past prices, technical analysis is a futile endeavor. An investor would gain more from a simple buy-and-hold strategy because in the long run the stock market in the United States shows an upward trend anyway. A buy-and-hold strategy involves buying a stock and holding onto it with the expectation that its price will rise in the future. Some studies have compared technical analysis tools with the simple buy-and-hold strategy and have shown that the buy-and-hold policy gives greater returns than trading based on technical analysis or trading rules. Technical analysis or trading rules tend to require frequent buying and selling depending on market movements. According to these studies, the chief reason for poorer returns from trading rules is that frequent trades have significant transaction costs. One must pay the broker high fees for every transaction. However, if one is buying and holding for the long term, one does not trade as much and pay as much in transaction costs. Technical analysts would tend to dispute the findings of such studies, claiming that trading rules are too complicated to be tested statistically. There are thousands of possible trading rule combinations depending on different situations, and a test cannot capture the richness of all trading rules. In addition, the studies done on technical analysis perhaps were done in the era before direct access trading when technicians would have to pay exorbitant brokerage fees. Now that the transactions costs are significantly lower than before, evidence against technical analysis and for the weak-form EMH may be less strong. Another point worth noting is that most of these studies that tend to confirm the weak form look at stocks that are traded heavily in the stock market. Any stock that is traded heavily is also a stock that would be followed closely by investors and information about which would tend to be more publicly available. As a result, it also would be a stock where arbitrage opportunities (buying low and selling high) would be more restricted. Thus these studies are biased toward the weak-form EMH. Had they taken into account less traded, less known stocks, the results might not be so strong.

To judge the extent to which the EMH holds, we could focus on how investment analysts and professional money managers handling the funds of large institutional investors such as mutual funds are performing. Under the EMH, we would expect these market pros, armed with valuable industry information and years of insight into the market, to be unable to consistently beat the average market return. They might beat the market in particular years, but they should not be able to systematically reproduce success. Such individuals work with information on companies and the market that other investors also are aware of, and according to the EMH, they should not have an edge in the market. Studies have looked at returns resulting from recommendations of particular managers and compared them with average market returns. In most studies, managers do not appear to outperform the market once transactions costs (costs associated with advice, brokerage fees) are brought into account. In the case of mutual funds, it is usually observed that funds that do well in one year usually do not repeat that performance subsequently. In fact, many mutual funds doing superbly for a couple of years have been wiped out of the market because of massive losses in later years. It all seems a lottery, which essentially lends support to the EMH.

One can inquire into the impact of major economic news or such public information on stock prices. According to the EMH, such information should not have an impact because the stock price already should have it accounted for. One way to check for this is to see how a stock price reacts *after* some major announcement about the stock has been made public. Most studies show that such announcements do not cause prices to fluctuate beyond a few hours after being revealed. Announcements on macroeconomic variables such as inflation, unemployment, etc., prompt investors to act swiftly. However, a lot of information made public is uncertain or unclear to investors. For example, projected future earnings reports provided by investment analysts are inherently uncertain, and people may not be willing to treat such reports as the final verdict on a stock. Reaction to this type of information thus may be incremental as investors gradually gauge the situation and act cautiously.

Several examples of expected price movements exist in the stock market that would appear to cast shadows on the EMH. For example, certain movements in stock prices coincide with particular times of the month or the year and are accordingly labeled as *calendar effects*. Year in and year out, these effects just do not seem to go away. One such effect is the *January effect,* and another is the *weekend effect.* The January effect is the phenomenon that stock prices tend to fall abruptly in December and then rise back as abruptly in January. This apparently results from investors trying to avoid paying higher taxes on their incomes. Investors sell off stocks in December to show capital losses, and when January rolls around, they promptly buy back these stocks or others. This phenomenon creates a downward pressure on prices in December and an upward pressure in January. Believers in efficient markets would be puzzled by this phenomenon because where are all the investors who could make a neat profit by buying low in December and high selling in January? Private pension funds and other investment funds do not have to pay such income taxes. They do not appear to jump in the market and make use of this profit opportunity (which puts into doubt the tax-related explanation of the January effect). Entire books have been written on the January effect, and it remains an anomaly. The weekend effect is a fall in prices at the close of day on Monday compared with the Friday levels. This suggests a simple rule of thumb to make profits: Buy later in the day on Monday when prices are relatively low, and do not buy on Friday afternoon or Monday morning when prices are relatively high. This is another predictable way the market acts. There is evidence, however, that the weekend effect is not a bonanza for investors looking to make a killing once transactions costs are taken into account. Thus it does not really undermine the argument surrounding the efficiency of the market because investors cannot use this phenomenon to make high profits.

Under the EMH, a group of stocks in the market should not have consistently higher rates of return compared with the general market. In reality, stocks of small firms tend to exhibit higher returns than those of large firms. Small-firm stocks tend to be riskier than the average stock. Thus we would expect them to have higher returns to compensate the investor for the greater risk of holding them. This is so because if an asset is more risky, an investor will not hold it unless it gives a higher return. Small-firm stocks, however, offer higher returns than average even when adjustments are made for the risk factor. Advocates of the EMH argue that this phenomenon is overstated because many small firms disappear from the market because they are inherently unstable, but when looking at returns provided by small firms, we can only look at those which have survived in the market, and these, naturally, are the successful ones.

According to the EMH, market actors would not react more than warranted to "new" news, and therefore, all market corrections are justified. What, then, about obvious examples of overreaction? Academic work in finance shows stock markets to fluctuate with a frequency that is far more rapid than would be suggested by information on the intrinsic or fundamental value of stocks. Detractors of the EMH point to an event such as the stock market crash of October 19, 1987 to drive their point home that wild swings in the market do occur that cannot be explained away by rational investor behavior. Within a single month, the Dow Jones

Industrial Average plummeted by one-third of its value. Supporters of the EMH would contest this by saying that no matter what the level of intermediate-period fluctuation, eventually stock prices do move in the direction of their intrinsic values.

The strong-form EMH, by definition, appears very rigid, and of the three forms of the EMH, it seems most vulnerable to the test of reality. It states that privately held information such as insider information cannot help an investor make extraordinary amounts of money in the market because even such private information permeates rapidly into the market. This issue can be argued both ways. The Securities and Exchange Commission (SEC) has very tough rules and penalties to prevent insider trading activities, and every so often we read in the *Wall Street Journal* about some trader or other getting nabbed by the SEC. Regardless, in Wall Street there seems to be a "don't ask, don't tell" type of tacit understanding that insider trading occurs at least at small levels. However, it definitely is not a significant profit source, and information flow from the inside of a firm to the outside has become a lot quicker in the 1990s. The stock market specialists, of course, make above-average returns from their activities in the market, although apparently there has been a downward trend to their returns.

So far we have seen evidence that in some cases the market seems to adjust to new information very rapidly, making predictions about the future a futile endeavor. This would lend support to the EMH. In some cases, the speed of adjustment seems rather slow and even predictable, which runs counter to the EMH.

TECHNICAL ANALYSIS

Technical analysis is built on the fundamental premise that *prices move in trends that persist and are predictable* to the discerning investor. It is indeed a far cry from the rational expectations world of the EMH. It is perhaps better suited to an adaptive expectations type of world. Prices would move in trends if adjustments to stock prices take place gradually over time as information gradually seeps through the different levels of the investment community. Advocates of technical analysis believe that markets cannot adjust to new information immediately because investors have varying levels of access to such information. For example, suppose that a Wall Street professional investor has access to information concerning the merger talks between Exxon and Mobile before it gets to ordinary investors. This investor will act on the information first, and prices may evolve as a result of his or her actions. Then the rest will catch on, and prices will continue to adjust. This adjustment process gives rise to trends. Technical analysts believe that history repeats itself and that so do stock price patterns. By looking at the market closely enough, one can get a sense of how prices move. There are no fixed rules, however, for every contingency arising, and investors must make judgment calls based on their experience of past price behavior.

The market price of a stock comes about by the interaction of its supply and demand. Excess demand (more buyers than sellers) would cause a price to go up, and excess supply (more sellers than buyers) would cause it to fall. Looking at stock prices and volume is sufficient to give an investor a sense of the direction in which the market is heading because they are the best indicators of the supply and demand conditions, i.e., the vibrancy, of the market. Let's consider one simple scenario of the path a stock price can take. For example, if the price of Yahoo! stock is increasing and is continuing to trade very heavily, we can guess that there is strong demand for it. Its price probably will rise further. On the other hand, if trading slows down at a certain price, investors are losing interest in the stock, and we can expect its price to start moving in the opposite direction. Price would keep falling gradually. Interest in the stock would tend to increase as this happens. Suppose that at a certain low price buying volume increases substantially. A reasonable guess would be that interest in the stock is back. Investors probably think the price has fallen enough. This is a good time to buy because the heavy trading volume signals the end of the downward trend in the stock. As an alternative to selling high and buying low, you also could have sold your stocks short once you thought that the price had reached its peak and you believed it would continue to fall.

The technical analysis approach looks at minimal information in the market. Purists (fanatics?) would go as far as to say that they do not even care to know what stock they are trading. It does not matter whether it is Coca-Cola stock or Mocha Cola stock. All they need to know is the history of the stock's price movements. This view perhaps goes a bit too far. However, technicians usually are skeptical about the usefulness of additional information available to the general market. They do not seem to think that analyzing variables that fundamental analysis looks at is particularly valuable. They believe that the only way that such data would help one beat the market is when it is of superior quality compared with what is available to the majority of the market. Data such as this is hard to come by for ordinary investors, and usually by the time they have access to it, the market has already taken the information into account.

From the technical analysis perspective, all tangible and valuable fundamental factors that could determine a stock's value already would be incorporated into its price. Thus there is no point in looking at the financial statements of a company. Technical analysts also point out the unreliability and incompleteness of company financial statements. They argue that no standard procedure is followed in the development of such reports. Firms can choose from a variety of procedures to furnish their revenue, expense, and return figures. Furthermore, to the technical analyst, financial reports do not account for many intangible psychological factors that potentially can affect the future of an industry. Thus they would rather let others worry about financial statements and what the analysts say and instead concentrate on price and volume. These variables encapsulate everything: investor knowledge, investor uncertainty, and investor ignorance. The emphasis on following the price variable in the stock market perhaps has not been expressed with greater enthusiasm than by Robert Edwards and John Magee in *Technical Analysis of Stock Trends*, the first edition of which was published way back in 1948:

> The market price reflects not only the differing value opinions of many orthodox security appraisers but also the hopes and fears and guesses and moods, rational and irrational, of hundreds of potential buyers and sellers, as well as their needs and their resources—in total, factors that defy analysis and for which no statistics are obtainable, but which are nevertheless all synthesized, weighed and finally expressed in the one precise figure at which a buyer and a seller get together and make a deal. . . . This is the only figure that counts.

The supply of and demand for a stock are determined by a plethora of factors. The demand for a stock can depend on something relatively concrete like a published report of the company's financial health, but it also can depend on something less concrete such as the general mood in the market. All investors would agree that both rational and irrational factors coexist in the market and affect the supply and demand conditions that determine stock prices. Technicians, however, believe that impulsive thinking and imperfect information flows dominate the market to an extent that the market is in no real hurry to move to the equilibrium that rational behavior would suggest. To them, psychological factors far more complicated than the rational expectations explanation of human behavior must be brought into account to explain stock market behavior. We already mentioned how "mob instinct" or "crowd instinct" could at times significantly affect market outcomes. This is a point technical analysis stresses. Suppose that a particular stock is on an upward move. Investors see this and want to buy the stock, further increasing its price. Every price increase creates a feeling of euphoria among investors that because there is so much demand for the stock, its actual value must be even higher. Investors continue buying. The market easily can go into a frenzy, with price spiraling upward. Investors always can pick up on such trends to exploit for profit.

More sophisticated psychological factors than mob psychology also may be at work in the market. One important indicator technicians try to observe in stocks is their support and resistance level. Under the EMH, no such levels should exist because an investor should not be able to say anything about future prices from the past. In reality, however, at least in the short run, stock prices often tend to have ceilings above which they do not rise and floors below which they do not fall. This was explained in Chapter 2. It usually is psychological factors rather than cold, calculating analysis that drives this phenomenon. Let's try to see how. Suppose that at a particular moment in time investors bought a stock for $100 that subsequently falls to $80. Investors naturally would become eager to sell the stock without realizing big losses. If the stock price begins to recover from $80 and climbs upward, investors would monitor what is going on very carefully. When the price nears $100, they would try to get rid of their stocks and leave the market without making losses. As a result of heavy selling as the price reaches around $100, the price of the stock would not cross $100. Investors at large would see heavy selling as a signal that the stock is perhaps not worth more than $100, and the price would then tend to stabilize. If this process is repeated a few times, the investor-imposed upward bound on the stock of $100 would become established. The inverse process would lead to the existence of support levels, i.e., price floors for stocks. Technical analysts believe that one can profit by trading based on knowledge of such predictable phenomena. One should sell as the stock price approaches its resistance level and buy as the price approaches its support level.

A criticism of technical analysis is that price patterns may not recur. A stock price may break free from a so-called resistance level, and a trading rule that did not anticipate this could cause investors to suffer significant losses. Thus trading rules based on certain predictions of price movement are not guaranteed to always succeed. This is a shortcoming that reasonable technicians would tend to concede. They would argue that any investor should be ready to take such hits when they happen because they will happen. They believe that disruptions to trends are not very regular features and that as long as technicians are following trading rules consistently, they will win out. It was mentioned in the last chapter that technical analysis is as much an art as a science. The same information can have different implications to different investors. One technician might look at an upward trend and think it is about to end, whereas another might think it will continue to rise some more. Given their different interpretations, they will act differently. Thus no trading rules are written in stone. This is why technicians feel it is important to follow price patterns carefully over time to minimize the risk of being wrong about the market. The more one knows about price history and patterns, the better discretion one will be able to use in trading.

Some detractors argue that the success of technical analysis has to be its downfall. Suppose that a particular trading rule is said to work. More and more people naturally would adopt it in the hope of profiting from it. This would quickly cause the profits from such a rule to disappear. The rationale behind technical analysis is that since prices adjust slowly, there are ample arbitrage opportunities in the market. More people using a specific trading rule would cause rapid price adjustments, undoing such arbitrage opportunities. In the stock market, nothing fails like success. Everyone mimics the success story, and then too many cooks have spoilt the broth.

The difference between the EMH and technical analysis lies in different world views. The former is a view based on the rationality of investors and the efficiency of the marketplace. The latter, conversely, views humans as being more mercurial and less mechanical, which leads to market imperfections. Exploiting market imperfections caused by human idiosyncrasies is the technician's goal.

FUNDAMENTAL ANALYSIS

We have already discussed fundamental analysis while explaining the semistrong-form EMH and technical analysis. The opinions of these approaches are not always very sympathetic to it. In this section we try to give you a deeper sense of what fundamental analysis is and what its potential shortcomings might be.

Many people are inherently skeptical of technical analysis because they feel that it tries to predict too much from too little. Fundamental analysis looks at a broad set of variables to ascertain the *true* or *intrinsic* value of a stock. Every stock has an intrinsic value that depends on how much profit the company will make over time. In this sense, fundamental analysis is a "back to basics" approach. A firm's actual potential can be measured by observing its present health and its expected future outlook. Many "fundamental" factors—present and expected future conditions of the aggregate market, the industry, and the company—need to be analyzed for this. Once these factors are taken into account and the intrinsic value of a stock is estimated, the result is compared with the prevailing price in the market. At any particular time a stock price may not mirror its true value. Sooner or later, however, it will, as people find out more and more about the actual conditions of the company. Thus the estimated intrinsic value can be used as a benchmark toward which the stock price should gravitate. Suppose that after extensive research the investment advising company TazDawg, Inc., has determined the intrinsic value of stock ABC to be at $40 per share. If its market price is $45, then the stock can be considered overvalued. Sooner or later the market would find this out, and the stock price would fall. Therefore, an investor who owns stock ABC should sell it now. If the market price were to be at $30, which is lower than the intrinsic value, the stock would be undervalued, and its price likely would rise in the future. This is a good time to buy. The investor using fundamental analysis is more interested in the long-term prospects of a particular stock while making trading decisions. The technical analyst, on the other hand, cares only about short-run arbitrage opportunities.

One important qualification must be mentioned. Although every stock has an intrinsic value, the best one can do is to estimate it. Present variables may not be complete and fully accurate, and the future, however predictable, is inherently uncertain. Calculating intrinsic value is not all science; it involves subjective judgments of assumptions involving the future. As a result, there is really no such thing as a unique intrinsic value. Different analysts would come up with different values based on different considerations or weightings of relevant factors and different assumptions about the future. Thus one analyst might project IBM's annual growth in sales to be 5 percent for the next 5 years, whereas another might project it to be 4.5 percent. Based on this, they will come up with different estimates of the intrinsic value of IBM stock.

Let's now look at how fundamental analysis can be used to estimate the intrinsic value. A stock's *intrinsic value* is the present value of the company's stream of future earnings and dividend payments. By holding onto a stock, an investor would get certain amounts of dividends from the company every year. Also, the stock price would appreciate or depreciate depending on how the company is doing. Each year a certain amount of wealth (positive or negative) would accrue to the investor. The total benefit of holding onto a stock is the sum of the benefits that accrue to the investor each year. The present-value concept is important because it brings into account the fact that the value of earnings in the present is greater to an individual than equal earnings in the future. This is so because we would prefer to receive $1 today than $1 next year. If we kept that $1 in bank, we could get interest of, say, 3 cents on it. This is in a sense the price the bank is paying us for not using that $1 today. We would be indifferent between getting $1.03 next year and getting $1 today. The present worth of that $1.03 today is $1. Alternatively, the present worth of $1 that we get next year is roughly 97 cents ($1 divided by $1.03). The present-value formula discounts future earnings by the interest rate, and the further an earning is into the future, the greater is the amount by which it is discounted. Thus, if we would get $1 two years from now, its present value today would be roughly 94 cents ($1 divided by $1.03 squared). The present value of holding a stock is thus the total of all future earnings discounted by the interest rate to convert it into how much it is worth to you today.

Prestigious Wall Street firms have developed extensive models to forecast the worth or potential of firms. This is why major investment banks have divisions named *equity research groups* that have a host of individuals doing research to forecast the intrinsic value of stocks. Of the variables these trained professionals look at, the more important ones are the expected growth rate of a company, standard company financial indicators (the price-earnings, or P/E, ratio, net profit margin, book value per share, etc.), a stock's expected dividend payouts, the stock's riskiness, and aggregate market conditions such as the future growth rate of the economy.

Expected Growth Rate of a Company
Commonsense thinking would suggest that the stock price of a company will be higher the higher its expected future growth is. One way of look-

ing at the expected future growth rate is to look at the dividend growth rate patterns. These patterns ought to be weighed by when in the future they actually take place. Let's consider two separate paths for stock ABC's dividend growth rate. Under one scenario, suppose that it grows at 10 percent for the next 3 years and increases to a 30 percent growth rate in the following 3 years. Alternatively, it could grow at 15 percent for the next 6 years. Which growth pattern would provide greater returns? We need to use a discounting formula to weigh the two. The finance profession has developed a mathematical formula named the *dividend discount model* (DDM) to calculate intrinsic stock values based on expected future dividend growth rates.

Standard Company Financial Indicators

Most practitioners of fundamental analysis, however, prefer to look at company growth in terms of growth in earnings rather than growth in dividends. For this they turn to company price-earnings (P/E) ratios. A low P/E ratio implies a more profitable stock because it has high earnings relative to its price. Fundamental analysis would suggest that investors buy this stock instead of one with a higher P/E ratio. P/E ratios are examined to compare stocks with one another. All other factors being the same, investors should buy a stock with a lower P/E ratio. Research also could project a stock's future P/E ratio. A declining ratio would imply that the stock will become more profitable over time. In this case, investors should buy it now.

Other than the P/E ratio, company financial statements include numerous other performance indicators. The *net profit margin* is an index calculated by dividing net income by total sales income. This ratio shows the profit potentials of a firm by showing how much profit it makes from an additional dollar of sales. Thus a net profit margin of 20 percent means that for every dollar in sales, a firm earns 20 cents in profit. Another index used to evaluate a company's financial health is its *book value per share,* which is the ratio of the company's net assets divided by its number of outstanding shares. If this value is higher than the company's stock price, then it could be interpreted as a signal that the stock is underpriced and that investors should buy it. Companies come up with a host of other financial performance indicators that are part of their financial statements.

Expected Dividend Payouts

Much in the same way as expected dividend growth, a stock's expected dividend flow can be used to determine the intrinsic value of a stock. In this case also, the rule is easy. The higher the present value of a stock's dividends, the higher is the price investors will be willing to pay for it. Thus, if an investment analyst upgrades a stock based on an expected dividend flow increase, investors can expect its price to rise, and they should scramble to buy it.

Riskiness

Another important determinant of a stock's value is its riskiness. Fundamental analysis looks at risk profiles of stocks to make investment decisions. Very few human beings love risk (although every one of us has at some time or other bragged that we are risk lovers). For the most part, human beings are risk averse. The typical investor would only buy a risky stock if its expected rate of return is much greater than that of a less risky stock. Otherwise, why not go for the safer bet? Thus, if two stocks were to have similar returns, a wise investor would buy the less risky stock. Moreover, if a stock suddenly became riskier, investors would pay a lower price for its purchase. For example, there is an index called Moody's that ranks countries based on their risk profiles. If Moody's were to declare that investing in China this year is risky due to the political climate there, investors would be hesitant to invest in companies with massive operations in China, and the stock prices of those companies would fall.

Aggregate Market Conditions

So far we have looked at company-specific performance indicators used in fundamental analysis. Broad economic indicators also affect the value of stocks. Suppose that corporate bonds in the market are offering handsome interest rates. The values of ordinary stocks are likely to fall as a result. The market is a place with so many choices open to investors that a change in any one issue surely affects the relative values of others to some extent. Thus, if the interest rates GM bonds are paying were to go up, many investors would flock to GM bonds in the hope of a safe and reasonably high return. This would depress the price of ordinary stocks. An example of a broad macroeconomic factor affecting the stock market is a government tax cut. This would signal that consumption spending would go up, subsequently increasing the demand for Procter & Gamble products. The value of Procter & Gamble stocks thus would rise.

From an intuitive standpoint, fundamental analysis can be very appealing because it looks at the basic factors affecting the intrinsic value of a stock. Shortcomings of fundamental analysis arise from two directions. First, as mentioned earlier, estimations of the true value of a stock may be off depending on assumptions made about the future. The second criticism comes from the EMH (to be precise, the semistrong-form EMH). Fundamental analysis is based on information that is public knowledge. Investors would adjust immediately to this public information, and profit opportunities would vanish instantaneously. Gains from fundamental analysis would be minor.

Let us first discuss the challenges to estimating the intrinsic value of a stock. A lot of resources go into careful analysis and predictions of stock values. Unfortunately, the intrinsic value is a concept that can change from minute to minute. One major unforeseeable event can negate carefully calculated estimates. Forecasting earnings is a difficult task as it is. One must estimate the size of returns and their timing. A lot of discretion is used in making assumptions to compute these estimates. The proper discount rate to be used in the valuation of stocks is also difficult to decide on. Changing the projection of a firm's future growth potential slightly can change the intrinsic value we assign to its stock. Apart from the fact that analyst discretion can affect stock valuation, another possibility to entertain is analyst error or incompetence. Even experienced analysts have been known to make mistakes or show bad judgment.

Calculations in fundamental analysis are done on the basis of the financial accounts of firms. We mentioned in the last section that technical analysts are skeptical of such accounts. Such skepticism often may be valid. A somewhat extreme example of this is what happened in the year 2000 to Micro Strategy, a management information systems consulting company. The company inflated its yearly revenue by calculating it as its expected revenues from all new projects over the next few years. This made the company look far more vibrant to the public than it actually was, and its stock climbed rapidly. Later the accounting discrepancy was detected, and the company's value plummeted rapidly. Valuation of Micro Strategy stocks based on its financial accounts would have been incorrect if very close attention were not paid to details. Accounting manipulations on a much smaller scale, such as creative ways to deal with matters like asset depreciation, tax shelters, and investment expenditures, can put into doubt stock valuations analysts come up with.

So far we have discussed the problems that can arise from calculating the intrinsic value of a stock. If the computed value is not accurate after all, then the market would figure it out and not gravitate toward it. Anyway, lots of unforeseen events can change the intrinsic value, making its search like looking for a black cat in a dark room when the cat is not even there. Believers in rational expectations would go a step further than saying that the search for an intrinsic value is flawed because it cannot be calculated within a reasonable degree of precision. They feel that the intrinsic value of a stock is simply its present price. So why search for it? Predictions by analysts are based on present and past variables that are public information. All such information has already been incorporated into the stock price, and thus there is no point in trying to compute intrinsic values or predict future prices. If this were the case, what are all these high-paid professionals in investment advisory firms getting paid for? Studies have been done to judge the performance of professional investors in beating the market. One such study was conducted by Burton Malkiel, the author of *A Random Walk down Wall Street*. He analyzed the investment performance of 19 Wall Street firms and found that their predictions of future prices based on sophisticated analysis were not really much more accurate when compared to future price forecasts based on simpler analysis. Also, analysts in general failed to beat the market consistently. Other subsequent studies also have claimed that after transaction costs are brought into account, professional money management funds or mutual funds do not offer above-average returns in the market. This is somewhat surprising given that these are institutions that frequently have access to new information first and yet fail to capitalize on it.

CONCLUSION

This chapter has provided the reader with a broad overview of the three schools of thought on investor behavior. The EMH is the approach that considers investors to be extremely rational and the market to be very efficient. Prices change in ways that are unpredictable. As a result, the best guess of the future price is merely the present price. One might as well be memory-less in the market and be no worse for it. Investors are unlikely to consistently make above-average money in the market by following technical or fundamental methods. Investors would be as well off investing in indexed stocks as in taking advice from investment gurus or professional money managers. One could even be brave and have a monkey pick stocks by throwing darts at a dartboard containing the stock names.

Technical analysis argues that weaker forms of investor rationality govern the market. As a result, prices do not adjust swiftly but move in patterns, and profits can be made by looking at price patterns and associated trading volumes. To technical analysts, the EMH is a very cynical view of the investment world. Fundamental analysis assumes a stronger form of investor rationality than technical analysis. Unlike the EMH, proponents of fundamental analysis believe that there is value added in looking at past and present variables to predict the intrinsic value of stocks.

Academic research generally has found technical analysis and fundamental analysis to be of limited value once transactions costs are brought into account. Nevertheless, both technical and fundamental analyses continue to be used by investors in the market. We get a lot of mixed signals from out there, and it is perhaps hard to reject any approach out of hand.

4

PRICE FORMATIONS AND PATTERN COMPLETION

TECHNIQUES FOR DETERMINING TRENDS IN MARKET PRICES

So far we have seen the fundamentals of technical analysis and why many individuals feel that using the methods of technicians works. In Chapter 2 we saw the basics of technical analysis, the people who use it, and the jargon of technicians. In Chapter 3 we looked at the issue of whether technical analysis brings any fundamental value to the investor, i.e., whether it works. These two chapters have provided us with a solid foundation on which to base an examination of the elements of technical analysis, which we begin in this chapter.

As we saw in Chapter 3, market theories and predictions are as varied as the market participants themselves. Some are fleeting, whereas others become classics and enjoy widespread use among market participants. With the wide variety of both market participants and theories employed by them, very few accurate generalizations can be made about what a good indicator of market behavior is, except for the most important one. That is, we can assert with relative certainty that everyone in the market is watching one indicator of trading activity—the price. Stock prices are the most important statistics of market activity, and watching them is the first issue that we will consider.

It may seem obvious that we should watch prices and that everyone watches prices as a signal of market activity because prices, by construction, are what investors are most interested in. That is, investors ultimately are interested in buying at lower prices than they sell or selling short at higher prices than they buy back, so of course they look to prices. Technicians look more deeply than at the current price. They look to where the price has been for guidance about where it may be going.

Technicians watch the market because the basic premise behind technical analysis is that there is a mechanism that drives prices, which we may perhaps think of as the *market mentality*. This mechanism pushes prices in one direction or another, and technicians try to decipher where those prices are headed. The term *mechanism* is appropriate here because the market's behavior has many facets to it. On the one hand, prices stumble around in a seemingly random fashion, like a mad person stumbling around in the dark. And yet, as Shakespeare said, it is madness, but there is a method to it. The method is seen in the cyclic and repetitive expressions of market behavior. In this sense, the market behaves like the weather; while it is random on a day-to-day basis, technicians believe that it moves in cycles, like the weather moves in seasons. And as such, perhaps it can be forecast with some accuracy, much like weather forecasters attempt to do.

Thus technicians look for signs of a changing mood in the market through the movement of prices. When we plot prices across time, we are plotting, as stated in previous chapters, equilibriums at which sellers agreed to sell and buyers agreed to buy. When we see prices gyrating up and down, we are seeing market participants trading identical shares of stocks at different prices simply because some time has elapsed. That is, technicians look for evolution of the market climate, an evolution that is manifested in the fact that people in a 5-minute, 1-day, or 1-week interval are trading stocks at prices that are different than they were in the previous minute, day, week, or whatever the time interval may be.

The question becomes how to recognize the mechanism at work. Technicians believe that an important contribution to the fundamental supply and demand conditions of the market is made by the fear and greed of market participants. That is, whether a stock price is increasing is related to how many people show up to the marketplace looking to buy versus the number of people who show up looking to sell, as well as how hard the buyers haggle with the sellers versus how desperate they may be to buy. Technicians argue that these factors are governed by cycles of optimism, greed, pessimism, fear, and so on. As a result, if the market's prices are governed by these emotions and these emotions move in these sorts of cycles, then the market as a whole will move prices in cycles that may be predictable.

Here enters charting of the most important statistic—price. Because the market is so big and has so many different participants, the entire group cannot move as quickly as, say, a single individual. The market as a whole must develop a consensus or unified movement among its many different participants. Hence the cycle of market movement takes time to play out. Technicians attempt to look at price movements to infer where the trading is pushing the market and how the profile of stock prices will play out over time.

DISCERNING THE MOVEMENT OF STOCK PRICES AND THE TREND

As we saw in Chapter 1, technicians describe the general movement of a stock price as a *trend,* which is a fixed direction. Trends can be upward, sideways, or downward. Put together, the three directions allow for a cyclic movement of stock prices. Figure 4-1 presents an example of a general sideways trend, or rectangle, followed by an upward trend and then another sideways trend.

The stock in Figure 4-1 is graphed over a long period of time (about 5 years), so most of the short-term fluctuations are shown. The only movements that we can see are the long-term movements. If we look at a much shorter range of data, such as in Figure 4-2, we can see the short-run and even daily volatility, but we do so at the expense of the longer, more drawn out trends, or the "big picture." In technical analysis, the longer the time span, the easier it is for the technician to discern a trend.

Sometimes the movement of stock prices is compared with sound waves, with minor waves surrounding each large movement. The tech-

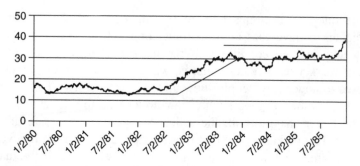

Figure 4-1 A sideways trend, an upward trend, and then another sideways trend.

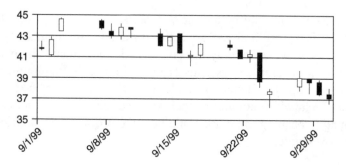

Figure 4-2 Candlestick charts showing daily volatility, but the primary trend is not as clear.

nician must look for the primary trends and discard the minor movements around it, which are sometimes referred to as *noise*. For example, Figure 4-3 shows the major movements of a stock price, with the minor movements drawn around it. The minor movements are short-term trends that do not last, and they fade as a larger time sample is graphed.

There are a few simple rules of technical analysis regarding trends. First, when presented with any doubt, it is assumed that a trend is continuing until there is sufficient evidence to assume that it has changed. This means that technicians only adapt to a new trend at the point where there is enough evidence to believe that a change in the trend has occurred. If there exists a reasonable doubt as to whether a change in the direction of the stock price has occurred, the technician will continue believing that the current trend is still valid. Thus, for example, if the market is rising and there is a small downward turn, the technician generally will not abandon a long position because of this. Only after suffi-

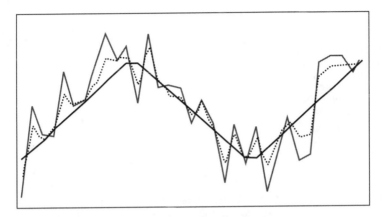

Figure 4-3 The main trend is hidden behind noisy short-term price fluctuations.

cient indicators show that the market has bearish momentum will the technician turn bearish.

The technician must wade through the information about a stock price as it comes in and determine if the stock price is continuing on its trend or suddenly changing direction. If the stock's price is increasing and then starts moving sideways and forming a rectangle, this is where the technician looks for clues of the next major movement. When a stock's price is increasing, then forms a rectangle at the top of a hill, and then falls, the rectangle is called a *distribution area* or *distribution pattern.* If the stock's price is falling, then forms a rectangle at the bottom of a valley, and then increases, this is called an *accumulation area* or *accumulation pattern.* Figure 4-4 presents examples of each.

In some cases, a stock may be increasing (or decreasing), then form a rectangle or trend sideways for some time, and then continue increasing (or decreasing). Since the stock did not change direction, the rectangles cannot be called distribution areas (or accumulation areas) because there was no reversal. As a result, these rectangles are called *consolidation patterns* or *continuation patterns.* In these patterns, the price of a stock pauses before continuing upward or downward. Figure 4-5 presents an example.

The idea behind an accumulation pattern is that as the stock's price falls and reaches its local low, smart traders will accumulate the stock and take the long position as the stock's price begins to climb up again. It is at this point that a strong buying presence in the market spurs on a

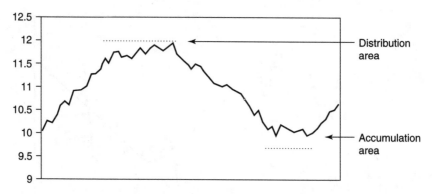

Figure 4-4 An example of a distribution area, where a stock's price stops increasing and falls, and an example of accumulation area, where a stock's price stops falling and turns bullish.

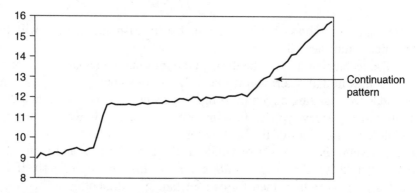

Figure 4-5 A continuation or consolidation pattern forms as a stock's price increases, pauses, and then continues increasing. The same could occur if the price were declining.

reversal. The price hits a support of traders who accurately or by luck perceive a strong enough buying presence in the market and an impending price breakout. Similarly, in a distribution pattern, the smart traders are unloading their long positions and acquiring short positions because the stock's price has reached its local high. As a result, the selling presence in the market is sufficient to impose a resistance price level on the market, and enough traders sense a strong selling presence in the market to cause a downward break in the rectangle. As the sell-off ensues, the price precipitates.

In a continuation or consolidation pattern, however, the bulls or bears pushing the trend cannot be stopped. In the case of a bull run, the price is increasing and then stops and trends sideways in a rectangle. At this point, the upward buying pressure subsides temporarily because perhaps the increase in the price has made a number of investors nervous about a possible reversal or that the stock price has gone too high, and they should take profits at this point. Another reason the price may stop increasing is that it hits a previous low or a previous support. Here many investors may have taken long positions, or bought stock, in anticipation of the stock increasing. The stock's price may then have continued downward, and these investors began losing money. Now, as the stock's price returns to the previous support level, the investors close their positions for a net zero gain, and some may even sell short in anticipation of another downward break. Whatever the reason for it, when the price that was in a bull run begins to trend sideways, the selling presence has increased and the buying presence decreased sufficiently to stop the price from rising. At this point in the consolidation pattern, stock is changing hands from those who believe its price will fall to those who believe its price will continue upward. When the stock breaks, its price may continue much higher because some of the sellers in the consolidation pattern may have sold the stock short in anticipation of a fall in price. When the fall does not occur, they will buy frantically and push the price up violently to cut their losses as soon as possible.

TREND OBSERVATION IN DATA

To observe a trend, obviously, the easiest way is to allow for the maximum amount of data points possible. The reason this works is that as more data are observed, each observation serves to confirm the general movement of prices, and a pattern is observed more easily. Detecting a trend is like trying to figure out which horse is going to win a horse race. Right out of the gate, all the horses are side by side, and one may be able to make an educated guess as to which will win, but looking at the horses running does not really add much information. The longer one watches, however, the clearer it becomes as to which horse will win the race. Of course, in some exceptional circumstances, one horse will break out clear in front of the pack from the very beginning. Similarly, in some cases, a price will shoot straight in one direction or another, and there will be little doubt as to which way it is moving. Even in these cases, however, it is not an open and closed case for the technician. First of all, if it is so clear that the price is taking a particular direction, it is self-evident not only to the technician but also to every other market participant. This would be the same as if in the horse race one horse pulls ahead by two lengths right out of the gate. Everyone will likely believe that the horse has a good chance of being the winner. Hence it is observationally clear what the trend is in cases such as these, and the technician's advantage is diminished. Second, if we consider the example of the horse race, the fact that one horse pulls ahead at the beginning implies nothing with certainty. What matters is which horse pulls ahead at the end. Watching the race longer will confirm whether that particular horse will maintain its lead, or whether one of the other horses will come from behind to win. Similarly, a stock may shoot up or plummet, but a sudden reversal may be right around the corner for that stock, making the trend a temporary reversal. For these reasons, having more data makes the determination of a market trend easier.

The technician then must decide how long or how far back to look for data. Obviously, the farther back he or she goes, the more accurate will be the general trend. On the other hand, going back to the year 1900 and drawing a trend leading up to last week is not of much practical use for investors. Just because the direct access trader invests in "the market for the next 100 years" does not mean that the trader wants to wait that long to get his or her money back. As a result, technicians choose a window of data that is appropriate for both their techniques and investment goals. If one wants to day trade, for example, intraday charts are crucial, whereas 1-year charts are of little use for the day trader.

Having the data plotted, the technician may proceed to draw a trend line using some basic techniques. When a stock's price is increasing, the line that depicts the general trend should cut below the low points as an upward-sloping support (Figure 4-6). When a stock's price is decreasing, the trend line should skim the tops of the highs as if it were a downward-sloping resistance line (Figure 4-7). Furthermore, one should not make the mistake of drawing a trend line from left to right when plotting stock prices. Many people begin looking at charts from left to right because they are accustomed to reading and writing from left to right. The problem is that when plotting stock prices, the most recent date is the most accurate depiction of market conditions. Thus, beginning to draw a line from left to right and using a point way off to the left of the chart are exactly backward and the exact opposite of what technicians recommend. One should begin drawing from right to left. In doing so, the most recent date is used correctly to anchor the trend line. Next, one picks out particularly outstanding days or prices.

Furthermore, when drawing a trend line, technicians often go about choosing the points through which to draw the line not only as a high,

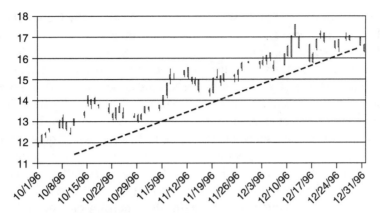

Figure 4-6 A trend line for IBM. The idea is to join the increasing lows in the run.

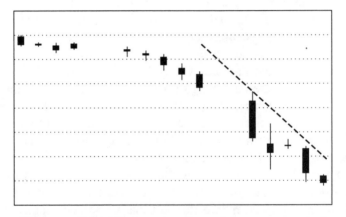

Figure 4-7 A declining trend line (IBM), drawn as a downward-sloping resistance. In this case, the market was tumbling because these data are taken from the crash of 1987.

as above, but rather as a high that is higher than the adjacent data points on the chart. That is, the line is drawn through highs that are higher the preceding and following days on the chart. With this technique, the points used for the line extend past the adjacent points on the chart. The intuition behind using these points is that they are more likely to be points indicating the eventual market direction than the adjacent points. In the case of an increasing market, for example, the trend line is drawn through points that are lower than their adjacent neighbors on the chart. These represent points in which the price attempted to fall and rebounded and continued upward. Hence these points reinforce the notion of an increasing market in that the price was not allowed to fall below them but rather pushed in the direction that the trend line indicates. In the case of a declining market, the line is drawn through highs that are higher than their adjacent neighbors. In this case, the market resisted an increasing price and pushed it back down. Hence these are points that serve as evidence for a declining market and reinforce the declining trend line.

Further improvements on a trend line can come through line correction. This technique, interestingly enough, is used when drawing lines from left to right but correcting for the fact that as new data come in, the new data are extremely relevant, so the line corrects for the data.

Figure 4-8 shows the trend lines rotating out and correcting for incoming data. The technician looking at this chart on or around June 13 would readjust the lines into July until it was sufficiently clear that the market had reversed and turned bearish. This is obvious to us because we can see well into August in this chart. The technician, however, must correct the trend lines to make the best estimate. Even if the trend had not turned bearish, as occurred in this example, technicians generally will correct their trends as new data come in, especially if the trend is indicating a sharp increase in prices. Generally speaking, if stock prices shoot up very quickly at the beginning of a prolonged bull market, the rate of increase in the beginning of the run is not indicative of the general rate of increase. As the market enters a period of expansion in stock prices, many market participants will rush to take long positions, and more important, those with short positions will buy to cover their positions and cut their losses as fast as possible. Obviously, for traders covering their shorts, it does not make sense to wait, nor will there be as many people in a short squeeze further into the bull market as there logically are in the beginning. These individuals will push prices up frantically and possibly cause the steep ascent in prices that occurs at the beginning of the bull market. For this reason, technicians will correct their trend lines so that they reflect more accurately the long-run growth rate.

Sometimes technicians draw a trend line below and a return trend line above for ascending markets or a trend line above and a return trend line below for falling markets (Figure 4-9). These lines together make a sort of channel for the stock price to travel through. It is like an upward- or downward-sloping rectangle. The return trend lines serve as guides for unusually strong moves. They are not as significant to the technician as are the normal trend lines but are used in conjunction with many of the signaling formations that we will cover in the rest of this chapter.

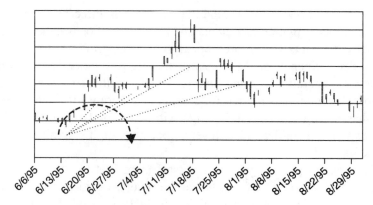

Figure 4-8 The corrective trend line shifts further until it is evident that the line needs to be re-drawn completely and the trend has undergone a reversal.

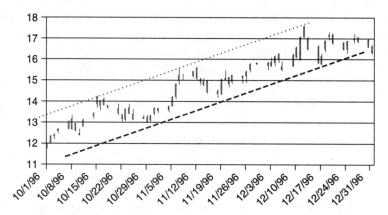

Figure 4-9 The trend line is the line below the data, and the return trend line is the line above the data, because in this example (IBM) we are looking at an increasing market.

REVERSAL FORMATIONS

Having established a trend line and how to identify it, we now turn to the all-important topic of how the market signals that it is ready to abandon a trend line. That is, we now look at stock price formations that show up on charts at times and signal to practitioners of technical analysis that a reversal may occur. Two general reminders about reversals are appropriate here. The first is that the longer a trend has been in effect, the stronger is that trend, and the more embedded it is in the markets. Thus, when a reversal occurs on a trend that has been in effect for a long time, it is a significant market movement and one that will be watched by many market participants. These present substantial opportunities for direct access traders. When a trend that has existed for a week or 10 days suffers a reversal, generally speaking, this is "small potatoes" for the market as a whole. If a trend has existed for 5 years and there is clear evidence that there has been a reversal, the market will adjust much more to it. Since the trend is so significant, the reversal becomes highly significant to the market as well.

The second point regarding reversals in market trends concerns the strength of the trend itself and hence the required evidence for the technician to consider that a reversal has in fact occurred. If a trend is a particularly weak trend, for example, because it is very steep, especially very steep and upward sloping, then it is not sustainable anyway. It is normal to expect the market to pull back from a sharply increasing trend. The reason is that a sharp and prolonged increase is unsustainable; it is a bubble, and the market will not support prices when the consensus is that they are artificially inflated and there is no value behind them whatsoever. This is exactly the situation behind a market that shoots up like a rocket. Trends such as these fade quickly into the past. Downward trends can be steeper because there are times when people sell off in waves of panic. This can allow for a reasonably steep trend in a falling market. Prices cannot spiral downward perpetually, however, and soon bargain hunters should eliminate overly steep falling markets, although not as quickly as overly steep bull markets. Given that one is not looking at such a situation, however, there are some trends that are strong, and if they are to suffer a reversal, the reversal must be strong as well. These are trends that have been tested by the market many times. Suppose that trend line number 1 for an upward market goes through 100 points on the chart and trend line number 2 goes through 5 points (also for an upward market). Trend line 1 is much stronger than line 2 because it has stood 20 times more tests as a trend. For each time the price attempted to break through line 2, the price tried to break through line 1 20 times. As such, the market has absorbed line 1 into its mentality in a much more profound way. After so many times of supporting the price at trend line 1, the market almost automatically will expect the price to be supported continuously at that level. As a result, every time the price approaches trend line 1, market participants will buy and take long positions and hence reinforce the same trend line again. In the case of line 2, the trend has not been as tested. Each time the price approaches the trend line, the market will look to the trend with much more skepticism. Since no one knows how strong the trend is, any approach is a potential reversal, and so many more people will be willing to bet that the market will break the trend. And of course, if sufficient people bet that the trend will be broken, this is exactly what will occur.

We now look at formations that appear on price charts, which are also called *price patterns* by technicians. The idea behind finding these patterns is that as they develop, if a technician can see them, then he or she is observing evidence of a reversal occurring. The term for this is *pattern completion.* If a technician sees a pattern completed, and the stock turns against the prevailing trend, then he or she has evidence that the primary trend has changed. Having observed a pattern completion, the technician usually will wait a short amount of time to see if the reversal holds and then invest, or wait to see if the price moves a certain amount or percentage, depending on what his or her personal preferences are toward risk. The sooner he or she invests based on a pattern completion, the sooner the technician will begin reaping profits if in fact the trend did undergo a reversal. On the other hand, a technician who invests right away each time he or she thinks a pattern has completed may invest many times erroneously, because the primary trend does not reverse. In the erroneous investments he or she will pay commissions and lose money, so the technician must guard against such mistakes while at the same time trying to get in on the legitimate trend reversals as early as possible. The patterns that signal follow.

HEAD AND SHOULDERS FORMATIONS

Probably the most well-known formation that signals a reversal is the *head and shoulders formation.* It occurs when a stock price rallies three times in a row, with the middle rally being larger than the first and third rallies. All three rallies should begin around the same trend line, which is called the *neckline.* Because the middle rally is higher than the two adjacent rallies, it is called the *head,* and the other two are called the *shoulders.* A head and shoulders formation is bearish and signals that the trend indicated by the neckline will be violated after the third rally. Figure 4-10 shows what a head and shoulders formation looks like.

Note that since the head and shoulders formation occurs on an increasing trend line and causes a decline, the classic situation in which a

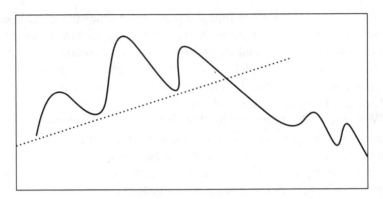

Figure 4-10 Head and shoulders formation. The two smaller rallies make up the shoulders, while the middle, larger rally makes up the head. The neckline indicates the trend that ultimately is violated after the third rally.

head and shoulders formation is present is at market tops and market bottoms. This, however, need not be the case. A head and shoulders formation can occur at a locally increasing point, even though the general market trend is downward or upward. Recall that technicians use formations to analyze different ranges of time, so the local market top may be part of an overall declining market. Figure 4-11 presents two examples of an inverted head and shoulders formation evident in an overall increasing market. Thus, in these examples, the inverted head and shoulders formation signals not a market bottom but a local bottom where the stock begins to increase again after falling locally.

More specifically, just as the head and shoulders formation indicates a market reversal, technicians also look for an *inverted head and shoulders formation.* In this case, the stock price would form a triplet of depressions or drops in which the middle drop is deeper than the adjacent two drops. Inverse head and shoulders formations work exactly the same as regular head and shoulders formations. Because one has to read the chart upside-down to see the formation, it is easily missed and frequently ignored. Figure 4-12 presents an example of an inverse head and shoulders formation.

Figure 4-11 shows a somewhat volatile but increasing market. Recall that head and shoulders formations signal a drop in stock prices after three consecutive rallies. Thus one would not immediately identify a head and shoulders formation in this graph because it is missing a key ingredient—the drop in stock prices. If we take a second look at the same

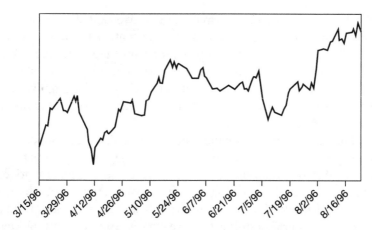

Figure 4-11 Two examples of head and shoulders formations (JPM). These formations may be missed, however, because the market is generally increasing.

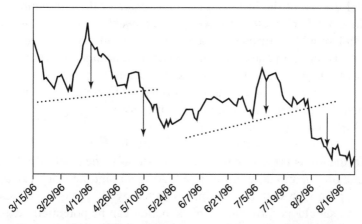

Figure 4-12 Notice the formation of the two shoulders and the head just above the trend line right before the stock price (JPM) moves to the bottom of the chart. Here the prices are inverted so that a move toward the bottom is an increase in the stock price. This is an inverted head and shoulders formation.

graph but now with the prices inverted, it becomes easier to identify the two examples of head and shoulders formations.

In Figure 4-12, by inverting the vertical axis so that the biggest price is at the top and the smallest is at the bottom, we can see our bull market for stock JPM now as a bear market and, consequently, more easily identify the head and shoulders formation. The two dotted lines signify the necklines, and the small shoulders are adjacent to the larger head formation. This market is moving up, with an inverted head and shoulders formation marking each major step of the increase. Again, notice that these inverted head and shoulders formations signal not a market bottom but a continuation of the same bullish trend that has local bottoms where the market increases.

Technicians facing a situation in which a head and shoulders formation is present await one of two scenarios. The first is that the predicted reversal of the formation materializes, in which case the stock price falls after the third rally of a head and shoulders formation or climbs rapidly after the third depression of the inverted head and shoulders formation. In this case, a natural question for investors is: How far will the reversal go? That is, given that the neckline has been violated, how far will the stock price travel past it? The arrows in Figure 4-12 indicate the answer that technicians provide to this question. The distance between the neckline and the top of the head is a rough estimate of the minimum distance that the stock is projected to travel past the neckline. This works for both head and shoulders formations and inverted head and shoulders formations. Thus, once a penetration of the neckline occurs, the technician will expect the price to fall at least the same distance as the top of the head in the preceding head and shoulders formation. Sometimes this price level is called the *minimum price objective*. It is a sort of target that the price should go to and possibly exceed.

Of course, the alternative scenario is one in which the head and shoulders formation is present, but after the third rally, the stock penetrates the neckline only marginally or not at all. At this point the stock price is not following through with the decline predicted by the price objective of the head and shoulders formation. This situation can be potentially explosive because if after the third rally the price only falls back to the neckline and the market rebounds, then the stock could be in for a potentially strong advance. The market here has not formed head and shoulders as a distribution pattern but rather has formed a continuation pattern. That is, the price does not fall but rather stays at around the same level. The head and shoulders formation is a distribution pattern because it distributes stock from profit-taking investors to investors taking unprofitable long positions at the start of a decline. Similarly, the inverted head and shoulders formation is an accumulation pattern because profit-seeking investors accumulate stock to take long positions before the stock price begins to climb. If either the rally or the decline of an inverted or regular head and shoulders pattern fails to materialize, then they are just continuation patterns. Investors who sell short or take long positions based on the existence of these formations will augment the market fundamentals that caused the failure of the head and shoulders formation. That is, head and shoulders formations occur when the market is ready to turn around and move the price in the opposite direction. This is why it is a reversal formation. If a head and shoulders formation does not lead to a reversal, then technicians assume that the market fundamentals are not pointing to a reversal. In effect, the market is not ready to push the price back the opposite way; it is not ready for a reversal. If, for example, investors sell short in anticipation of a reversal that market fundamentals do not support, they will be caught in a short squeeze, and when the price increases, they will further push the price up, causing an amplification of the increase that the fundamentals are calling for.

VOLUME

Often on financial news programs or business reports commentators mention daily volume and heavy or light trading when describing whether the market moved up or down. They do so because a description of the market conditions without consideration paid to the market's trading volume would be severely lacking. The role of volume in the markets and in technical analysis cannot be understated. The market's *volume* is the number of shares traded each day. Thus, for example, if on a given day only one share of stock was sold on the market, that day's volume would be 1.

The importance of volume lies in the fact that it is a measure of the participation of the rest of the market and consequently signals, among other things, the depth of the market. To understand the role that volume plays in predicting reversals, and for technical analysis in general, we can think of what a technician would see and what the decision-making process would be like based on a market in which information about volume were not available.

The technician in this case would see only a price moving around and fluctuating on the market. Granted that knowing where the price was 10 minutes or 10 days ago relative to now, and 10 years ago relative to now, is important. The problem for the trader, however, is that there is no picture of the market as a whole for him or her to see. Seeing volume allows the trader to have another view of what is generally going on in the marketplace. It is not unreasonable to assume that traders in a market all have different opinions about the value of a stock. For example, some traders may be bearish on a stock, whereas others are bullish. Some market participants know more about the value of a company's stock than others. For example, some market participants may learn important information about a company's stock before the rest of the market. If situations such as this occur, then it becomes useful to know what others in the marketplace are doing. By looking at volume, the technical analyst gets a glimpse of how many people are interested in a stock and how active the market is. Technicians look to volume to see if others are acting on a trend, if others in the market are participating in and pushing a reversal, and what sort of interest there is in a stock.

Normally, technicians expect volume to be increasing when the price is increasing and decreasing when the price is decreasing. This relationship between volume and price is a regularity that has been observed and has come to be expected by technicians. Some have explained this phenomenon as a result of the fact that while price is increasing, the profitable position to take is to go long, or buy the stock. The profitable position to take while the stock price is falling is to go short, and sell the stock short. In the market, however, it is much easier to buy stock than it is to sell it short because broker/dealers place restrictions on short sales, as do the rules of the marketplace. The Nasdaq, for example, restricts short sales to upbids so that traders are prevented from selling into a falling market. Since there are no such restrictions on taking the long position, it is natural to expect more people to take profitable positions in bull markets than in bear markets. As a result, volume should be heavier when the market is increasing than when it is falling. There are other explanations for the increasing price–increasing volume, decreasing price–decreasing volume phenomenon, explanations based on information problems, for example. The problem is that intuitively there is no reason to think that because there is heavy trading, the price should be increasing. It could be decreasing during heavy trading as well, and in fact, it does many times.

Technicians believe, however, that volume and prices move together and that with increasing prices, we have increasing volume. They take volume to be an important signal of possible changes in activity. For example, during a head and shoulders formation, technicians would like to see decreasing volume to reinforce the head and shoulders prediction of a reversal. Since head and shoulders formation forms on an upward trend, the technical analysis expectation for volume is an increasing volume pattern. Hence, as price is increasing, if volume is falling, a technician will expect some sort of a change to occur because the expected pattern is being violated. In addition to this, if a head and shoulders formation is present, then a technician has evidence supporting a downward turn in the market.

Note that volume is not measured in absolute terms for technicians. In the marketplace, volume is an idiosyncratic feature of a company's stock. Thus, for example, a company that is very heavily traded and very well known, such as Microsoft or General Electric, will function in normal or even light trading with much more volume than a small and insignificant penny stock. In this situation, the technician obviously will not look to see what the volume is but rather what the volume is relative to what it may have been in the past. Hence, just as a technician looks at the price on a daily chart, the volume is plotted right below price so as to show the relative changes in volume and how the market is evolving in terms of shares changing hands for that stock while the price is rising and falling.

GAPS

Besides looking at the historical profile of a stock price and the volume at which the stock traded, technicians also look at the intraday volatility and the range of prices at which the stock traded. The *intraday volatility* consists of the changes in price that occurred within a single day as a by-product of the trading of the stock throughout the day. This information is important because, like volume, it describes the atmosphere of trading on the market. In a sense, the intraday volatility describes how the herd of traders is moving the price. For example, suppose that the price of stock XYZ opens at $30, increases to $180, and then falls to $7 before recovering and closing at $32. Now suppose that the price of another stock, call it stock ZYX, opens at $28, trades to a high of $31, and closes at that high. The trading range of stock XYZ is much larger than that of stock ZYX. Technicians use this information to identify stocks that are on the move and that are poised for a strong breakout in one direction or another.

Now suppose that a stock skips trading at prices along its trading range. In previous chapters we identified this as a gap. That is, a *gap* occurs when a price skips price levels on its way up or down. Technicians watch for gaps in price charts because they indicate a strong bearish or bullish tendency in the market depending on the underlying trend and because it is generally accepted among technicians that the price will return and trade at the levels that were skipped by the gap. Thus a gap in a bull market indicates that the market participants were so eager to buy that they pushed the price up faster than they could trade, and as a result, trades did not need to occur at some levels because some people did not bother to sell at these levels. Sellers in a bull market with a gap did not have to sell at price levels that were skipped; they just found buyers at higher price levels. This is why technicians believe that gaps reinforce the bullishness of a market. If a gap were to occur in a declining market, the same would be true of buyers who simply waited for the price to fall rather than buying at the levels that were skipped by the gap, because the sellers were so desperate to sell.

There are three kinds of gaps that technicians look for in charts. The first is a runaway gap, the second is an exhaustion gap, and the third is a breakout gap. A *runaway gap* is a gap in trading that occurs when a market is rising too fast or falling too fast, and price levels are skipped (Figure 4-13*a*).

An *exhaustion gap* occurs at the end of a particularly sharp advance or decline in prices. The price jumps but then discontinues its previous ascending or descending trend and enters a rectangle. The reason this gap is called an *exhaustion gap* is that it comes at the end of a very pronounced movement, and the price stops moving after the gap. It is as if the market is exhausted either from climbing so high and so fast or falling so low and so fast that it gaps but then stops climbing or falling for a while (see Figure 4-13*b*).

Once the price shows an exhaustion gap, where it is in a sideways market at the bottom of a decline or at the top of a rally, it will continue to trend sideways until a breakout occurs. When this happens, if in the process of breaking out the price gaps, i.e., jumps out of the rectangle formation so fast that it skips price levels, this is called a *breakout gap*. Thus an exhaustion gap comes at the end of a rally or decline and leads to a sideways market, whereas a breakout gap makes the price exit the sideways market in abrupt fashion and begin to climb rapidly or descend rapidly (see Figure 4-13*b*).

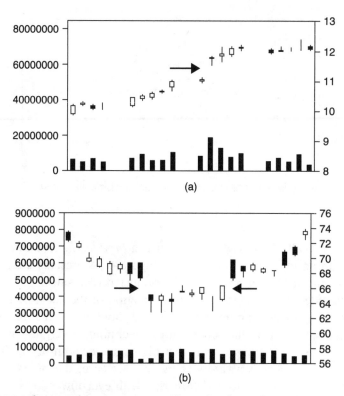

Figure 4-13 (*a*) The arrow shows a runaway gap. The market skips trading at these price levels on its increasing trend. (*b*) The arrow on the left shows an exhaustion gap that comes at the end of a decline. The price then sits in the island rectangle formation until the breakaway gap, which is pointed out by the arrow on the right.

BROADENING FORMATIONS

The next formation we will look at combines volume analysis with the idea of a head and shoulders formation. It is called a *broadening formation*. The broadening formation signals a reversal to technicians in the same way that a head and shoulders formation does. In fact, broadening formations are exactly like head and shoulders formations, except that instead of having three rallies, with the first and third rallies about the same size and the intermediate rally larger, the broadening formation has three or more rallies with each subsequent rally larger than the preceding. That is, in a broadening formation, the neckline is still increasing as in a head and shoulders formation, but the highs of the rallies are all in-

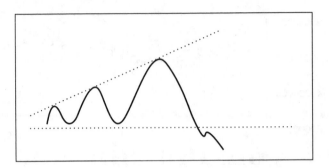

Figure 4-14 A broadening formation. The price is projected to violate the support.

creasing as well. This is why it is called a *broadening formation.* There are ascending tops and a flat support. Figure 4-14 presents a diagram of a broadening formation including the projected reversal.

A broadening formation signals a violation of the neckline to a technician. Just as there is an inverted head and shoulders formation, a broadening formation also can occur with a declining, diverging trend line. That is, instead of having ever-higher highs, one or both of the diverging trend lines can be downward-sloping. In this case, the broadening formation is documenting a bearish market with ever-lower lows.

Volume for a broadening formation is expected to conform to the usual assumptions. That is, for the case where the broadening formation is predicting an upward breakout in price (in the case of the market seeing ever-lower lows), the volume should increase with the breakout. That is, higher volume should accompany the higher prices predicted by the broadening formation. This would be the case of a broadening formation with a downward-sloping trend line connecting the bottoms of the price depressions. Here the broadening formation is signaling a price increase, which makes it an accumulation formation. We would expect an increase in volume with the violation of the resistance in such a situation.

In the opposite scenario, where there is an ascending trend line connecting the tops of the rallies (as in Figure 4-14), the broadening formation is predicting a market downturn. As a result, the volume should decrease with the price decline. If the volume increases with the violation of the flat trend line, however, this may not necessarily mean that the price will not continue to fall. The broadening formation would be serving as a distribution pattern in this case because the stock is being distributed away from investors who are aware of the impeding price decline. Recall that we mentioned earlier that volume could be very large at times when stock prices are falling. Hence, if volume picks up, the formation could be signaling a nosedive for the stock price.

DOUBLE TOPS, DOUBLE BOTTOMS, TRIPLE TOPS, AND TRIPLE BOTTOMS

The double-top and double-bottom formations are similar to a broadening formation, except that volume plays a key role here. The *double-top formation* consists of two rallies of similar size, one right after the other. The key feature is that the volume on the second rally is considerably lower than that on the first. If this formation occurs, it signals a reversal and a downward breakout to a technician.

Figure 4-15 shows a double-top formation. This example underscores the utility of volume for technicians. By noting that the second rally occurs on light volume, a technician can identify a weakening bull market. The market has twice tried to separate itself from the support, and both times was drawn back. At the end of the second rally, the price drops below the support. Since the price level has penetrated the support, the technician expects price to level out at a distance below the support at least as large as the tops of the rallies.

Figure 4-16 shows a double-bottom formation. Again, the volume is the key to identifying a double bottom. The decrease in volume from one depression to the next signals the double-bottom formation. Once the price penetrates the resistance level, technicians expect the price to continue upward as far as it climbed from the bottom of the trough to the resistance level at minimum. The arrows in the figure indicate this distance. Triple-bottom and triple-top formations are just a variation of double-bottom and double-top formations with one more trough or rally. The implications for volume are the same for the third trough or rally. That is, technicians expect that volume will continue to decrease into the third rally in the case of a triple top or into the third trough in the case of a triple bottom. This formation can include quadruple tops or quadruple bottoms, and as long as the volume is increasing in each subsequent trough or rally, the reversal implications are the same.

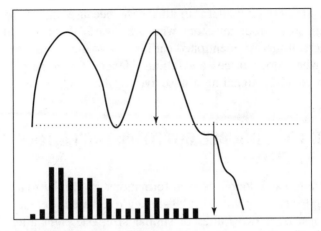

Figure 4-15 A double-top formation. The stock price will show two very similar rallies, but the second rally will be formed on much less volume.

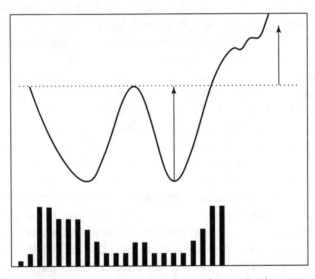

Figure 4-16 A double-bottom formation. Volume increases as the price breakout penetrates the resistance level. It is estimated that the increase in price corresponds in size to the rally from the bottom to the resistance level at minimum.

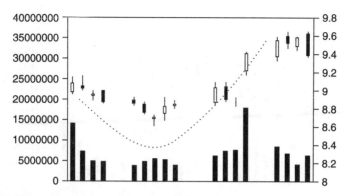

Figure 4-17 An example of a saucer formation with the predicted upward breakout in price. The dashed line shows the saucer-shaped nature of the formation.

SAUCERS

Saucers are like double bottoms without the double. A *saucer formation* is a price-volume combination in which the price forms a trough and the volume does as well. That is, the price falls, stops falling, and then recovers and increases. In the meantime, volume decreases, stops decreasing, and then increases. A saucer formation is depicted in Figure 4-17.

In this figure we see an example of a saucer formation in which the volume decreases and then increases. The formation's upward breakout is realized on heavy volume, and the price consequently increases.

ROUNDED TOPS

The rounded-top formation is similar to a saucer and a double-top formation. It is similar to the double top but again without the double. It is just one top, but it has the same volume characteristics as the saucer formation. That is, the *rounded-top formation* consists of a long, slow rally in which prices gradually increase and then fall, making a big fat hill. In the meantime, the volume is doing the exact opposite. It is decreasing slowly until it hits rock bottom just as the price reaches the peak of the hill. Then, as the price slides downward, the volume picks up. Figure 4-18 presents an example of a rounded-top formation.

The fact that volume is decreasing as price is peaking and then increasing as price is falling is suggestive of the bearish implications of this formation. Figure 4-18 gives an example of the rounded top and the

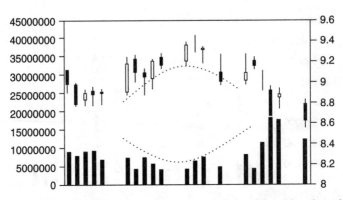

Figure 4-18 A rounded-top formation. The market increases and then falls, while volume does the opposite. This has bearish implications. The dotted lines show the rounded top and the U-shaped volume.

subsequent fall in prices. In this formation, the market loses interest in the stock as it gets expensive, but trading comes roaring back as the price declines.

TRIANGLES

There are three kinds of triangular formations or triangles. They are symmetrical triangles, ascending triangles, and descending triangles. *Ascending triangles* and *descending triangles* are the mirror images of broadening formations. Instead of prices fluctuating up and down in widening cycles, they fluctuate up and down in tighter cycles.

Figure 4-19 shows an ascending triangle, in which the price bounces in smaller cycles toward the level of resistance. It is generally believed by technicians that a formation such as this indicates an impending bullish breakout on the upside, as shown. That is, the ascending triangle indicates a bullish price increase on heavy volume once the resistance level is penetrated.

A descending triangle is a mirror image of an ascending triangle, as shown in Figure 4-20. A descending triangle formation has three sides. The bottom is flat, the left is vertical, and the top connects these two with a downward-sloping line. The price fluctuates within these lines in an ever-shorter cycle, bouncing off the support level but rising in a lower rally each time. The market is indicating that there is no will to push the price up higher. This formation indicates a bearish price breakout past the support.

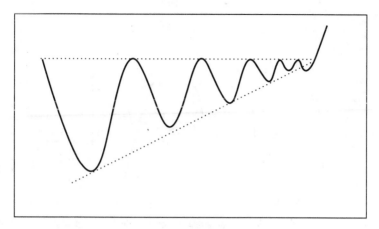

Figure 4-19 An ascending triangle.

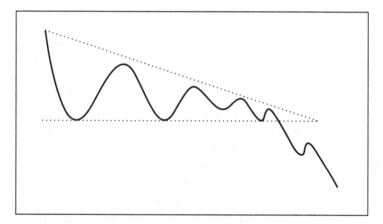

Figure 4-20 A descending triangle.

A *symmetrical triangle* is a formation in which there are a series of market cycles in which each successive high is lower than the preceding cycle's high and each successive low is higher than the preceding cycle's low (Figure 4-21). Here the market is in a clear battle between the bulls and the bears. There is no general consensus among technicians as to what a symmetrical triangle indicates. As the price fluctuates up and down, the bears and the bulls are exhausting their capacity to sustain a prolonged price movement. Hence technicians generally accept that in a symmetrical triangle, a breakout on the upside is a bullish indicator,

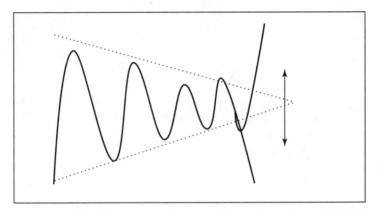

Figure 4-21 A symmetrical triangle is an uncertain indication as to the direction of the breakout, as indicated by the two possible breakouts and the double-sided arrow. Furthermore, if the breakout occurs too far to the right, the sustainability of the price breakout is called into question by technicians.

whereas a breakout on the downside is a bearish indicator. However, if the breakout occurs too close to the edge of the triangle, where there is minimal movement of the price, technicians are skeptical of the validity of this signal.

The symmetrical triangle highlights a problem that is present in all three triangular formations. This is that they are a clear manifestation of a battle between bears and bulls, which is the everyday business of the stock markets. For this reason, these formations appear very frequently in price charts. Sometimes a triangular formation is confused with a general rising market, and this can cause problems and mistaken buy or sell signals. For this reason, triangles are often considered unreliable. Clearly, a generally upward trend is not consistent with a triangle in that the flat support, for example, would not be present. Many traders identify what are called *upward-sloping triangles* and *downward-sloping triangles,* which are just ascending or descending triangles with a slanted support or resistance. The inclusion of these makes disentangling a triangular formation from a general upward or downward trend with even moderate variation difficult. Furthermore, the potential breakouts that these formations signal more often than not turn out to be just sideways trending and rectangular formations. As a result, triangles may be more trouble than they are worth and should be considered as light evidence of a potential breakout in one direction or another.

The formations we have seen so far serve as buy or sell signals for technicians, in that they are technical indicators of impending market reversals. As the profile of a stock price evolves into a market trend and more time passes, this trend is strengthened. The stronger the trend, the more profitable becomes the potential reversal. As a result, at each pause in a stock price evolution, technicians must consider whether a reversal is at hand. The formations just described serve as evidence in favor of a trend reversal occurring. The evidence of a reversal may fail the technician, however, in cases where the trend continues and the technician mistakenly bets his or her money on the occurrence of a reversal. In the case of a failure of one of these formations, e.g., the failure of a head and shoulders formation, the pattern serves as a continuation formation. These continuation patterns are where the market catches its breath before continuing on a trend. For example, a generally upward-moving price level characterizes a bull market, and in the general upward movement of prices there may be some temporary pauses. Such pauses are where the market stops to redistribute stock from investors who perhaps do not believe that the price can go much higher or who want to cash in their earnings to investors who perceive the increasing trend and are betting on a continuing upward movement. Hence distinguishing between a continuation and a reversal in a trend is important for technicians because during a continuation, technicians will let their money ride on the trend continuing, whereas if they believe a reversal is imminent, they will commit to the opposite strategy. The mechanism discussed next serves technicians for this purpose; i.e., they signal such continuations rather than signaling buy or sell to the technician.

FLAGS

Flags are well-known formations that occur in sharply increasing or decreasing markets. They represent the point mentioned previously where the market needs to catch its breath, so to speak. After increasing sharply, the price forms a sideways rectangle where the lateral trending is a redistribution area. The stock price drifts sideways while shares are changing hands between those nervous about the upward or downward spike and those betting on a continuation of the trend.

Figure 4-22 presents an example of a flag formation signaling a continuation. The dotted rectangle shows the sideways trending as the stock price drifts. Volume is generally decreasing along the lateral drift until

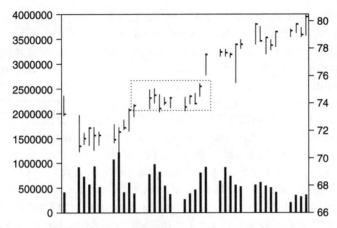

Figure 4-22 An example of a flag formation. It is a continuation formation with decreasing volume.

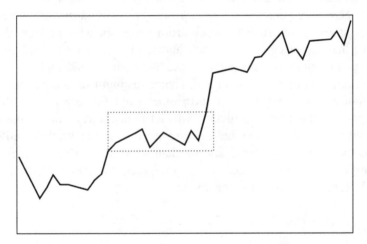

Figure 4-23 This is the movement of prices present in Figure 4-22 without the high-low-close chart or the volume. The rectangle is visible with this type of charting as well.

the breakout, where it increases to accompany the increasing stock price. The formation is called a *flag* because after the sharp increase (or decrease), the rectangle forms what looks like a flag on the chart. In the chart in this figure, the lines with the small pegs on the side represent the high-low-close prices of the day. The high for each day is the top of the line, the low for each day is the bottom of the line, and the small rectangular peg extending out from the right of each vertical line is the

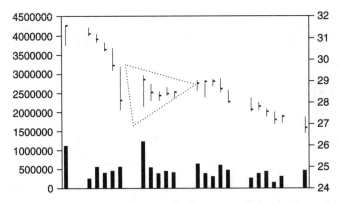

Figure 4-24 An example of a pennant. The triangular formation on declining volume signals the continuation area and the imminent downward breakout as the declining market trend continues after the temporary pause.

closing price for each day. These charts are especially prone to showing flags because they clearly show a rectangular formation on the days when the price is drifting sideways. The rectangle is still visible, however, without the high-low-close chart, as shown in Figure 4-23.

A flag on a decline will look the same as in Figure 4-23, except that the trend will be an overall declining one. The volume will decrease as well throughout the rectangle and may pick up on the downward breakout if the market is particularly bearish.

PENNANTS

A *pennant* is identical to a flag in all respects except for the rectangular formation formed by the lateral drift of the stock price. In a pennant, the stock price trends sideways in contracting cycles to form a symmetrical triangle. The volume implications are the same for a pennant as for a flag. That is, volume is expected to contract along the pennant, and if the market is increasing, volume is expected to jump when the upward breakout occurs (Figure 4-24).

WEDGES

A *wedge* is another continuation formation. It is very similar to a pennant. Figure 4-24 shows a pennant that has a triangular form, with the top leg of the triangle pointing downward and the bottom leg pointing upward.

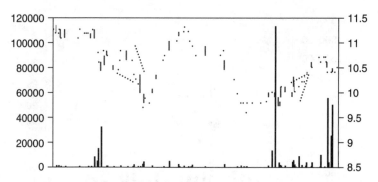

Figure 4-25 The formation of two wedges. Notice the sharp spikes in volume due to the wedge formation's inherent acceleration of market prices.

If instead this triangle had both the top and bottom legs pointing upward or both pointing downward while still converging, this formation would be a wedge, not a pennant. That is, a wedge is a triangle with two sides either increasing or declining while at the same time both converging. Figure 4-25 presents two examples of wedges. The characteristic of higher highs and higher lows present in a wedge formation makes its presence potentially destabilizing for the market. In an upward-sloping wedge, for example, the lows are increasing, as is each subsequent high. As a result, the market has the potential for an explosive price jump and an explosive reversal further down the line.

CONCLUSION

In this chapter we have looked at the formations that technicians use as evidence of the size and direction of future market movements. Use of these formations is predicated on the price repeating the same behavior in the marketplace that it has in the past. Technicians recognize that there is never a clear and simple indicator that appears and indicates a buy or a sell. These formations serve as evidence for the practitioners of technical analysis, but the weight of the evidence must be pondered carefully, and in the end, a judgment call must be made whether to heed what may appear to be a buy signal or what may appear to be a sell signal. For this reason, technicians look at many different forms of evidence on whether to buy or sell. In the coming chapters we will look at some of the other forecasting techniques used by practitioners of technical analysis.

5

THE DOW THEORY

The Dow theory is the pioneering work in technical analysis. In **Technical Analysis of Stock Trends** *(1948), Robert Edwards and John Magee rather humorously referred to it as the "granddaddy of all technical market studies." Although a little over 100 years old, its concepts are still the basis for many indicators that investors use in predicting the future movements of the stock market and of particular stocks. The theory is named after Charles Dow, the first editor of the* **Wall Street Journal** *and a founder of Dow Jones & Company.*

Technical analysis makes use of the fact that prices move in ways that are predictable. Dow also laid out certain tendencies or patterns of stock price movements over time. This is why the Dow theory is of particular interest to adherents of technical analysis. Dow described stock prices as following trends parallel to movements of seawater. Over time, stock prices follow movements that can be classified broadly as primary, secondary, and minor movements. The *primary trend* is the long-run trend of the market, which can be bullish or bearish. Over a long time horizon, the stock market would show an upward trend or a downward trend. This dominating trend is like tides. Followers of the Dow theory also believe that the market does not rise or fall steadily but suffers intermediate "hiccups," i.e., corrections in the opposite direction of the main trend. The *secondary trend* is the transitional movement of prices (i.e., the hiccups), which create resistance to the major trend. Thus the stock market might be rising in the long run, but in the intermediate periods it would move downward temporarily only to recover and move up again. This reversal phase is like waves. They are powerful but are overpowered by the surging tide. Finally, there are the *minor trends,* which are the everyday fluctuations in stock prices. These are inconsequential in the broader scheme of events. These minor trends can be compared to ripples. We discuss these three market trends in the next section of this chapter.

The *Wall Street Journal* made its appearance in 1889. Ideas surrounding the Dow theory appeared in Charles Dow's editorials in the newspaper during the years 1901 and 1902. Dow was among the first to believe that common stock prices and the stock market moved in discernible patterns rather than randomly. His editorials dealt with investment strategies in the stock market and were based on his personal observations of stock price movements over a period of 20 years. The ideas in his editorials came to be referred to as the *Dow theory* only after his death. Samuel Nelson, a publisher friend of Dow's, was an early enthusiast of his work. Within a year of Dow's death in 1902, Nelson wrote *The ABCs of Stock Speculation,* explaining Dow's ideas. This book also included 20 of Dow's original editorials, and it is in this book that the term *Dow theory* was coined.

Ideas surrounding the Dow theory were improved subsequently. Dow's successor as editor of the *Wall Street Journal,* William P. Hamilton, continued to write editorials based essentially on Dow's observations of stock market movements. For 27 years—from 1902 to 1929—he wrote editorials illuminating and improving on Dow's original ideas on price movements. He actually wrote much more on Dow's ideas than Dow himself did. In 1922 he published *The Stock Market Barometer.* It is Hamilton's work that we most closely associate with the Dow theory. Just months before his death in 1929, in one of his editorials, he predicted the end of the bull market that began in 1923. Another serious contemporary work that developed Dow's work was Robert Rhea's (1932) *The Dow Theory: An Explanation of Its Development and An Attempt to Define Its Usefulness as an Aid in Speculation.*

Dow's own ideas were about general market trends. When he spoke of the three major trends, he alluded to the stock market as a whole. He believed that the stocks of more reputable companies tended to move in the same direction. This was a belief shared by many other investors in the market at that time. In a bull market all prices would tend to rise, with some prices rising more than others. In a bear market prices would tend to fall, and some probably would fall more than others. This also tends to be the case if we look at the stock market today. In the 1990s, the market had been bullish, with majority stocks gaining in value, but technology stocks clearly led the pack with very high returns. There are stocks that are exceptions to this general trend, of course. There are prices that move in the opposite direction of the general trends. The price of oil is an obvious example of this. When the price of oil rises, production costs go up and the economy slows down. As a result, general stock prices fall. However, other than freak exceptions or commodities that are countercyclic with the market, in general we observe that stock prices move correspondingly. Dow used this observation to develop predictions as to general stock market movements. He believed that looking at price movements of stocks could give investors a sense of where those particular stocks were heading and where the market in general was heading. Moreover, since stocks tend to move in harmony, by looking at a select few stocks one could get a sense of the entire market. Keeping this in mind, Dow developed the idea of an index of representative stocks to act as a proxy of the general market health. This led to creation of the Dow Jones Industrial Average (DJIA) and the Dow Jones Railroad Average, later changed to the Dow Jones Transportation Average (DJTA). Dow considered a stock's price to reflect all the information that is available on that issue. All one could find out about a particular stock from sources such as financial reports, investor newsletters, television news, or a newspaper like the *Wall Street Journal* is reflected in a stock's price. Dow took the argument further by stating that *the market averages also reflect all the information that investors are aware of.* If this were true, the market averages would pretty much tell us all there is to be known about the market.

Today the DJIA is a list of 30 stocks, and the DJTA is a list of 20 stocks. However, the Dow averages have evolved a lot over time and continue to do so. When it first appeared in 1896, the DJIA was composed of 12 industry stocks. In the late nineteenth century, the market was not as developed as it is today, nor was it as active. There were issues that would sit idle for days. Some companies would just vanish suddenly because of bankruptcy. Stocks that would characterize the market properly were not easy to come by. To keep up with changing market conditions, the Dow averages were restructured every now and then. Over time, some companies were dropped from the index and others included. In 1916, the DJIA increased the number of stocks in its list to 20 because business activity in the United States was expanding rapidly and investor involvement in the stock market was rising considerably. In 1928 the number increased from 20 to 30, and it has since remained unchanged. The stocks that make up the DJIA, of course, remain in a state of flux as the index continues to choose stocks that apparently represent the general market. With the market structure changing over time, a stock that was representative of the market in the 1950s may not be so in the 1990s. For example, as technology stocks became more and more prominent in the 1990s, the DJIA finally included Microsoft in its listing. A firm may be dropped from the index because it has been bought by another company. On the other hand, a merger of two companies may make them such a significant industry player that the new company would be inducted into the DJIA. Of the original 12 stocks of the DJIA, only General Electric remains on the list today. The 30 stocks listed in the DJIA as of November 2000 are

3M Co.	Eastman Kodak	JP Morgan
AT&T Corp.	Exxon Mobil	Johnson & Johnson
Alcoa	General Electric	McDonald's
American Express	General Motors	Merck & Company
Boeing	Hewlett-Packard Co.	Microsoft
Caterpillar, Inc.	Home Depot	Philip Morris Co.
Citigroup	Honeywell International	Procter & Gamble
Coca-Cola	IBM	SBC Communications
Disney	Intel	United Technologies
DuPont	International Paper	Wal-Mart

The DJIA is composed of stocks that are major market forces. Thus, if the DJIA, also called *the Dow,* is doing well, it can be interpreted as a sign that the business atmosphere is healthy. If a Dow stock such as Procter & Gamble is doing well, it can be inferred that consumer demand for Procter & Gamble's products is strong and will continue to be strong. Other businesses would then feel rosy about the economy and increase their production. As a result, the Dow can act as a lever that pulls the economy with it. Of course, there are shortcomings to the Dow also because it is an index of only 30 players in the market. This is why many investors look at a broader index such as the Standard & Poor's 500 (S&P500, an index of 500 companies) index to ascertain business activity.

The original Dow Jones Railroad Average was made up of 20 railroad companies. Railroads were the leading mode of transportation for business products at Dow's time, and railroad companies were the most rapidly growing companies. Dow felt that the Railroad average was a crucial indicator of the economy and the stock market in general. It was through the railroads that raw materials were transported to factories for production, and the same railroads transported the final output to the market. In a more vibrant economy, greater production would take place, and transportation activities would increase. As profits of railroad companies would go up with increased business, prices of railroad stocks also would increase. Thus the *Railroad index,* as it was called, could at that time act as a barometer of the health of U.S. business. With the passage of time, the relative importance of railroads as a means of transport declined as road and air transportation facilities improved. In 1970, the Railroad average changed its name to Dow Jones Transportation Average (DJTA) and began to include airline and trucking companies in its listing. Besides the DJIA and the DJTA, there are other Dow averages as well. The Dow Jones Utility Average (DJUA), an index composed of utility company stocks, is one of them. Although it also is an important indicator of the market, this index is not closely tied to the Dow theory. Dow theorists feel that it is affected by many other important factors that are not necessarily related to the health of the economy and therefore cannot be used to judge it.

Charles Dow believed that the Industrial and Railroad averages should be followed jointly to try to ascertain the direction of the general market. This was because the Railroad average tended to track the DJIA. As business expanded or contracted, transportation activity would tend to go up or down with it. With greater business activity, the DJIA would tend to rise, and so would the Railroad average (presently the DJTA). Depending on how strongly or weakly the DJTA tracked the DJIA, we could make predictions as to which direction the stock market would be heading. If the two averages diverged, we would expect them to converge soon. *This tendency of the averages to converge is a central tenet of the Dow theory.* We will come back to this later in this chapter and see how the two averages can be used together to forecast future market movements. Another useful Dow concept relates to tracking the total volume of trade in the market. This volume can help investors track the strength or weakness of particular price movements. This idea by now should be quite familiar to you, but we will touch on it to see its relevance in determining whether the direction of the market is bullish or bearish.

The main concepts of the Dow theory can be stated as follows:

1 Stock prices and the market averages discount all information that is available in the market. Also, stock prices in general tend to move in the same direction.
2 The market has three trends: primary, secondary, and minor. The primary trend has three phases.
3 The DJIA and the DJTA must confirm.
4 Trading volume in the market tracks the direction of the primary trend in the market.

The first concept has already been touched on. In the remainder of this chapter we talk about the other three concepts, especially the three trends of the market. In addition, we also briefly touch on other Dow-related concepts such as line formation, double-tops, and double-bottoms.

THE THREE PRICE TRENDS

Stock prices in the market tend to move back and forth together. Depending on the state of business and the economy, the market tends to have an overarching direction of movement. If the economy continues to grow at a healthy pace with the business outlook looking rosy, the stock market continues to appreciate in value. If the economy suffers from a recession, stock prices depreciate. This occurs despite the periodic reversals and minor day-to-day fluctuations in a generally upward- or downward-moving market. Reversals may happen because the market is moving too fast for its actors to figure out what is going on. Actors then slow things down by being cautious and putting the brakes on the market.

After such periodic corrections, the market moves on again. Dow spoke of primary, secondary, and minor trends that make up the market movements. We now discuss these.

Primary Trend

Of the three trends, the primary trend is the dominating long-run trend of the market. When we talk about the market being bullish or bearish, we refer to the overall or primary trend, the DJIA being the market proxy. Dow believed the primary trend to last usually for a year and sometimes for more than that. In the present day, however, the market is a lot more fast-paced than it was about a century back, and a bullish or bearish trend may last only months. *For believers in the Dow theory, the primary trend is the most important trend for investors to ascertain.* An investor who can buy at the beginning of a bull market and sell toward its end stands to make a lot of profit. On the other hand, an investor who can sell toward the beginning of a bear market and buy toward its end also would profit significantly from the market. However, it is not so easy to figure out the beginning and ending of a bull or a bear market and time one's actions perfectly. In fact, it may be difficult enough to figure out whether the market is bullish or bearish at any particular time. By looking at the market closely, however, one can get a better sense of when it is bullish or bearish and when a particular bullish or bearish trend has begun or has ended. Thus, even if an investor does not catch the precise moment of the beginning or end of a bullish or a bearish market, he or she possibly can catch the trend soon enough to make significant gains.

As we mentioned earlier, the stock market does not rise continuously or fall continuously. It may rise for 4 straight days, fall for 3 days, remain steady for 1 day, and then rise for 5 days and fall again for 6 days. With the market oscillating in such a manner, going in one direction for some days then going the other way on other days, how can we tell whether the market is bullish or bearish? An investor is likely to be confused by looking at the market over a 1-week time horizon to figure out whether the market is bullish or bearish. For this the investor must look at market prices over a longer time horizon.

We know that each upsurge in the market tends to have an accompanying downward reversal. The Dow principle is that if each reversal is followed by an upsurge that takes the market to a higher level than before, then it is a bullish trend. Suppose that the DJIA rallies from 5000 points in March to 5500 by May. It then reverses to 5300 by June. If it begins an upsurge again in June and beats the 5500 mark, then we can say the market is bullish. Thus every subsequent peak must be higher than the previous peak. The opposite holds for a bearish market. As the market declines, periodically it will have reversals or corrections upward. As long as each decline following an upward reversal takes the market to a lower point than before, the market is bearish. Suppose that the market were to drop from 5500 to 5000 and then correct to 5200. Suppose that it subsequently fell to 4800. Then we would be in a bearish market because the new low (4800) is lower than the previous low (5000). These are very simple examples of when we can easily say something about the market. However, it is not always so cut and dried. In the same example, suppose that if after the correction to 5200 the market fell not to 4800 (below the previous trough of 5000) but instead to 5100 (above the previous trough of 5000). Now the fall in the market did not take the market to below its previous decline, because 5100 is greater than the previous low point of 5000. This puts into doubt the continuation of the bearish trend. It probably signals that the bear market is likely to end, and we would look at subsequent market movements to see that a bull market might be likely to begin. It is crucial to compare subsequent highs or subsequent lows with each other to decide whether an old trend is continuing to persist or is switching to a new trend. Looking at Figure 5-1 will clarify this.

The market is initially bullish as it moves from A to a higher level B. The market then corrects and moves downward to C. After enduring the resistance that pushed the market down to C (which is higher than A), it moves up again and peaks again at D, which is higher than B. The market therefore remains bullish.

From level D, the market reverses again to E. The upward movement from E to F now, however, fails to beat the previous peak D. The bullish trend is likely to be over. Whereas previously the upward movement was the primary or dominating trend, now it looks likely that it is the downward movement that is dominating. This is so because the decline from D to E outstripped the rise from E to F. Let's continue to follow the market. From F the market moves down to G, and this is at a lower level than the previous low point E. We can say that the bear market has almost surely started as the downward move continues to dominate. A role reversal has occurred. The downward price movement is now the primary trend, and the upward movement has become the secondary trend.

Let's now try to characterize price movements in a bull and a bear market. Suppose that the market is generally in an optimistic mood be-

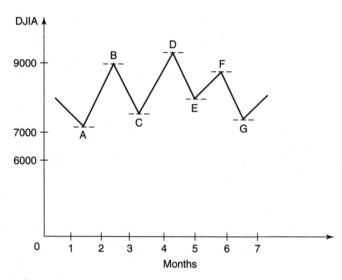

Figure 5-1 Market trends.

cause the signs for future business prospects are good. The Dow averages would tend to be on the rise. However, even in this generally optimistic period, the market would reverse itself occasionally for short durations. This is likely to be due to profit taking by investors. If stock prices reach a certain level, investors may feel that prices have risen enough, and they are not sure if they will reach higher. To be on the safe side, they may then decide to sell their stocks and take profits immediately. Large market movers such as institutional investors may have automated sell programs so that when a stock reaches a certain price, a vast amount of the stock is unloaded for sale in the market automatically. This would immediately cause the market price to move downward. This reversal in prices is what we have so far called the *secondary movement*. If the market health is sound in general, investors would realize that they acted a bit too soon by selling their stock. They would again want to buy the stock. With this increase in demand, the market would again be on an upward move. The market would thus alternate between periods of upward movement and reversals in the opposite direction. It becomes important to see the extent of rises and reversals to ascertain whether the market is bullish or not. If the rises dominate the subsequent falls, the market is bullish.

According to the Dow theory, *a primary trend has three phases.* A sustained bullish trend is likely to begin after a prolonged period of depressed business atmosphere. This is a period when prices have declined over a period of time to such a level that general investors have lost interest in the market. A number of discerning investors, however, foresee a better future for the market and feel that prices are low enough to start buying. To most investors, the market still may not seem to have a very healthy future, with business activity not showing any real signs of picking up. However, with some interest on the part of a relatively small number of investors in buying stocks, prices would slowly start creeping up. This is the beginning, or the first phase, of the bull market. Gradually, with the business atmosphere picking up, company revenues and profits would pick up also. This would be a period of steady increase of stock prices as confident investors continue buying. This is the second phase of the bull market. This phase might last for a year or more. During this time, both trading volume and price increases would go hand in hand, and the market would make sustained gains. Eventually, however, the market would slow down again as business activity overextends itself. There would be caution on the part of general investors. Prices would continue to increase because some investors would continue to remain optimistic about the future. While prices might remain high and occasionally rally, the rallies would become more erratic and less strong. This would signal the beginning of the end of the bull market and would be its final phase. Then the bear market would begin. While all bull markets are not the same, they tend to mimic the preceding characterization. The only differences probably would occur in terms of the relative strengths of each of the phases. Our neat breakdown into three phases is in a sense that of a classic bull market.

A bearish primary trend would follow the opposite path. The market generally would be moving downward due to a lack of excitement concerning the future prospects of the economy. As prices fall, at a certain price, investors may think that prices have dropped enough, and it may be a good time to buy. Institutional investors may place huge buy orders at such a price level. As they demand stocks at that price, the market would rise. This rise, however, would be short-lived because the overall projections for the economy are not very optimistic. The market would fall again to a lower level than before, and the bearish trend would continue. A bear market would begin where a bull market ended. It would start off with the secondary downward reversal becoming the primary trend. As the future continues to look dismal and business activities slow down, the downward movement in prices will grow stronger. Eventually, as prices keep falling, individuals who had held out in the hope that the market would improve may start selling out of fear and distress. This would cause the market fall to continue. This process will carry on until prices have reached a level where investors realize that prices are below their worth and start purchasing again. Notice that like the bull market, the bear market also could be divided into three phases. The first phase begins with the switch from the bull to the bear market as investors become less cheerful about the future prospects of the economy. The next phase occurs when business earnings are down, and the market outlook is truly bleak. Prices would decline steadily during this time. The final phase, which is the panic stage, occurs as investor pessimism and impatience reach their highest level, and investors unload their stocks in the market at prices lower than their true worth.

There is no magic formula by which one can predict when a bull or bear market will begin or end. One can, however, follow price trends by looking at charts and discerning the direction in which the market is moving. An investor who looks at a short time horizon and cannot figure out the primary trend should look at a longer time horizon. As long as an investor has figured out the primary trend of the market, he or she can make money by trading at roughly the right times. The secondary reversals or minor everyday fluctuations need not perturb the long-term investor.

Besides taking the help of price charts to figure out primary trends, investors also can look at a moving-average chart of the market. Moving averages are discussed in Chapter 6 in detail, and here we will just mention them briefly. A *moving average* is the average price of a security over a stated time period. Thus a 200-day moving average would be the average price of a stock over a 200-day horizon. Ordinary price charts may confuse an investor. Price movements are often too spiky, and a rapid rise or decline in prices can throw off an investor's attempts to determine the primary trend. Moving-average trend charts are smoother than ordinary price-movement charts. The day-to-day price of a stock would fluctuate a lot compared with its moving average because the moving average collapses the stock prices of a certain number of days into one price. Technicians can use the moving average of the DJIA as an indicator of the long-term trend in the market and compare the present DJIA level with it to look for changes in trends. The moving averages usually employed by investors to determine the primary trend in the market range from 4-week to 200-day averages. A 200-day moving average demonstrates investors' general idea of the price in those 200 days. If a stock's price is above its 200-day moving average, this would imply that investors are more optimistic about the market than they were in the last 200 days. Thus investor sentiment could be considered bullish. Conversely, if a stock price is below its moving average, then investors would tend to be bearish because they are more pessimistic about the market. The way investors use the moving-average concept for trading is as follows: If the present price (along with heavy trading) overtakes the moving-average line from below, investors would sense the arrival of a bull market and buy stocks. If the present price dips below the moving-average line from above, investors would predict the beginning of a bearish market and sell their stocks. There is more to using moving averages than what is described here. Also, a challenge is to decide what time length of moving averages to use in determining market trends. Such nuances of moving averages are discussed in Chapter 6.

Besides the moving-average line, there are a few other "quick and dirty" indices that an investor can look at to determine market strength, i.e., how bullish or bearish the market is. One such index is the *advance-decline (A/D) line,* which gives investors a sense of aggregate market strength. The market can be considered more bullish as more stocks advance in value than decline. One can compare the A/D line from one period with that of another to note the direction of change in the market: A fall implies a bearish market, and vice versa. Furthermore, one also could compare the A/D line with the DJIA to try to find out the market trend. For example, if the DJIA is climbing while the A/D line moves downward, it might be the case that the market is beginning to weaken. Although the overall market trend is positive at the moment, more stocks are moving downward, and this predicts a potentially weak business outlook for the future. Eventually, the DJIA is likely to correct and follow the A/D line. Thus we might be able to anticipate the change in the DJIA by looking at the A/D line.

Another index to judge market strength is to look at market *new highs and new lows.* On a given day, new highs are the stocks whose prices peak at levels previously not attained. Inversely, new lows are the stocks whose prices reach their lowest levels. The greater the new highs are compared with the new lows, the more bullish the market trend can be thought to be. If the difference between new highs and new lows narrows over time, this would tend to suggest a weakening in the market. Eventually, the trend may change. A sudden rise in the difference means that a more bullish market is likely. New highs and new lows provide a very general sense of the market. Investors must not depend on them too much, and this measure always should be examined in conjunction with the movements in Dow averages.

Secondary Trend

A secondary trend is a trend that impedes the primary trends. Secondary trends last from days to even a few months. In a bull market, secondary trends are the periodic declines or corrections, and in a bear market, they are the periodic price recoveries. We have discussed how the primary trend dominates the secondary trend. The secondary price reaction is always smaller than the primary price movement. As a rule of thumb, Dow theorists consider a secondary reaction to lie between one-third and two-thirds of its preceding primary movement. Thus, if the DJIA gained 300 points in a particular primary swing, the following secondary swing would cause it to decline by somewhere between 100 and 200 points. In a bear market, on the other hand, a 300-point fall would be followed by a 100- to 200-point recovery. There clearly is no mathematical formula or fixed logic behind this, but Dow enthusiasts feel that this usually tends to be the case in the stock market. While we said that primary trends are difficult to determine, so are secondary trends. It is often hard to make distinctions between primary and secondary trends, especially when a bullish or a bearish trend is about to end. What we might have thought of as being a secondary downswing in a bullish market actually may be a primary downswing signaling the end of the bullish market.

The secondary trend in a bull market chiefly results from investor profit taking. As prices reach a certain level, investors start selling huge volumes, thinking that prices have risen enough. Large institutional investors may have automated sell orders that get activated as the market reaches a specific level. This impedes the upward progress of the market as it faces resistance. In a strong bullish market, however, the market would be able to break free of this resistance. The general outlook of the economy being healthy, the resistance level would sooner or later be broken because investors in general are optimistic about the future. Besides investor profit taking, other factors also may lead to market correction. Suppose that the Federal Reserve (the Fed) raises the interest rate in response to fears of inflation in the economy. This would cause a dip in the market. If investors are appeased by the Fed's action and their inflation fears are allayed, the market would tend to rise again once investors feel that after all is said and done, the economy is on the right track.

In a bearish market, secondary reversals occur when investors engage in large-scale buying when the price falls to a certain low point. Large and influential institutional investors may consider this a good point to buy, and their automatic buy programs may go into effect. This price level is a sort of support level, which creates resistance to prices falling below it. Buying pressure at such support prices would cause the market to recover temporarily. The general health of business activity being bearish, the euphoria of market recovery would die down soon, and the primary downward trend would continue.

In a sense, secondary trends in the market are due to forces created by support and resistance levels. If these support and resistance levels are weak, then they are broken by the primary trends. If the market has difficulty in breaking a support or a resistance level, we can predict that the market trend is about to change. Let's look at the example in Figure 5-2 to see this. We are initially looking at a bull market. Suppose that the market rises to point A and subsequently declines to B as a result of investors selling off their stocks. From B it rallies to a higher point C. At C the market faces some resistance and fails to move up further. Again, a profit-taking phase follows, and the market gradually declines to D. The rally from D fails to beat the previous resistance level C and peaks short of it at E. The price turns downward from point E. In the subsequent rise, the market also fails to beat the resistance level at C. This is a signal that the bull market is likely to be over.

The secondary trend to a large extent can be the product of activity in the market by institutional investors who control massive amounts of assets. These institutional investors (pension funds, mutual funds, and other large investors) could cause certain support or resistance levels to come into play. Other market experts and investment gurus also may be instrumental in this. Suppose that a very influential expert predicts, based on his or her analysis and observations, that the market ought to be at a particular level. As the market proceeds to that level, investors may have a tendency to slow down and think twice. This is all it may take for a secondary trend to develop. If some market participants can affect prices to this degree, they may even be able to manipulate the market in the short run. In the long run, however, the market would follow its primary trend, which depends on strong forces such as the inherent strength of the economy and business activity. In the short run, however, the possibility of some form of market manipulation cannot be ruled out completely. It is easy to see how one could benefit from successful short-

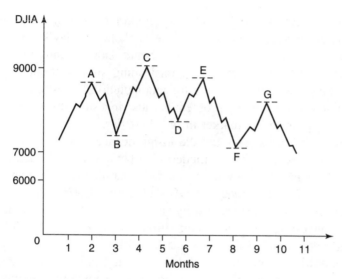

Figure 5-2 Secondary trends in the market.

run manipulation of the market. Suppose that a particular investment company unloads a heavy-duty selling program in a rising market. Other investors are also likely to follow suit, and the market would drop. The same investment company can then start buying again at the low price, and the market would be pushed up again. It is very hard for an investment organization to engage in willful manipulation because it is unlawful to do so. Nevertheless, the big players in the market can and do make markets move in desired directions in the short run. The general investor can, however, look at price charts of the market and have a sense of the way the market is moving and what the support and resistance levels are. While it is sufficient for long-term investors to follow the primary trend, it is essential for investors who trade more frequently to understand the secondary trends as well.

A useful way to ascertain the secondary trend in the market is to look at the DJIA and the DJTA together. We discuss this very important concept in the next section of this chapter.

Minor Trends

Charles Dow considered the daily movements in the stock market to be inconsequential in determining the state of the market. These movements, the *minor trends,* which last for a few days and sometimes may even stretch themselves up to 3 weeks, are important only because their aggregation is the secondary trend of the market. In today's stock market, minor trends may be as short as a few hours. Dow actually believed that the minor trends often could give misleading signals about the market because they are subject to investor manipulation. Investor overreaction is also a potential short-run problem because investors do not really know what is going on in the market in the short run.

Dow probably exaggerated the insignificance of minor trends, especially when looked at from a modern-day perspective. The market tends to react a lot faster to news, and market volatility is higher as a result. On October 19, 1987 alone, the DJIA plummeted 508 points, losing 20 percent of its value. This was hardly an inconsequential market movement for many investors who "lost their shirts" in the market. While it is increasingly common for the stock market to lose a few hundred points a day, events like the crash of October 1987 are still very infrequent. Investors can get some help from following the joint movements of the DJIA and the DJTA to form an idea of upcoming short-term movements or corrections in the market. At least they can get some warning signals if something major is about to change in the market.

Now that we have discussed all three of the market trends, Dow's metaphor of comparing market trends to the movement of seawater should make more sense. The force of the primary bull trend is like tides carrying seawater to increasing heights. The tides hit the shore and then recede, making waves. This reversal is like the secondary trend of the market. The tides continue to come in more furiously. Each tide overpowers its preceding waves to reach new heights. In the middle of this there are the tiny ripples and bubbles that are created in the water. These are inconsequential compared with the tides and the waves. They are like the minor trends in the market that really do not upset the other two trends. The tides cannot continue to reach newer heights forever, and sooner or later the retreating waves get more dominant. This would signal the end of the bull market and the beginning of the bear market. The reverse process would explain bear market trends.

THE DJIA AND DJTA MUST CONFIRM

So far we have discussed how an individual may follow a market index such as the DJIA in an attempt to determine the trend of the market. According to the Dow theory, following the market by observing charts of both the DJIA and the DJTA can give an investor a better sense about the sustainability of a particular primary trend. There is a theoretical reason for the two averages to track each other. The level of business activity in the United States affects the DJIA. As business production goes up, the DJIA soars. Transportation activities also increase in a flourishing economy, and this would positively affect the DJTA. In a sluggish business environment, both business and transportation activities would decline, and usually so would both averages. As a result, there ought to be some conformity between the two. Since industry and transportation complement each other rather than act as substitutes, there is no reason for the averages to run in opposite directions, except perhaps in the very short run when the market is still trying to figure out what is happening in the economy. Dow theorists argue that if the two averages do not conform at a given time, it is safe to predict that a market correction is in the offing. It is not the case that the two indices must track each other perfectly. There might be a time lag involved. Thus the DJTA may follow the general direction of the DJIA with a lag of a day, a few days, or even a week or more. The DJIA also may "correct" itself by looking at the DJTA.

From observation of the stock market it is evident that the DJIA bounces around more sharply than the DJTA. This is not really surprising. While the DJIA could at times depend on a host of factors that are rather tentative in nature (e.g., speculative bubbles), the DJTA would tend to be more closely tied to the actual performance of the economy. In this sense, the DJTA is a more stable indicator of the actual health of the economy. Thus, if the DJIA rises significantly but the DJTA does not rise at all, investors should doubt the strength and sustainability of the former's advance. In this case, the bullish trend is not likely to be very strong but rather is an upswing that would be corrected soon. The benefit of following the DJTA is that it can help us get a better sense of how strong a bullish or bearish trend really is. If a bullish trend is weak or coming to an end, the DJIA still may continue to go up, but the DJTA may tend to remain more sober. On the other hand, if a bearish trend is coming to an end, traders may go into a selling frenzy that plunges the DJIA down, while the DJTA may remain stable as investors there look at the actual economy to see that things are turning around. Let's look at the example shown in Figure 5-3 to understand how to interpret signals from a joint consideration of both the averages.

Let's assume that the market has been bullish for the last few months. From point A, the DJIA declines to point B and then rises to C. From C, it again falls to D. Compare points B and D. The fall to D has taken the

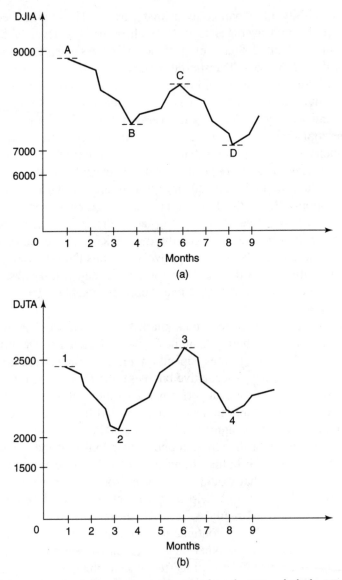

Figure 5-3 Interpreting signals from a joint consideration of (*a*) the DJIA and (*b*) the DJTA.

DJIA to a lower point than the previous low point of *B*. This would tend to signal the beginning of a bearish period. But let's see what the DJTA is doing at the same time. At around the same time it fell from point 1 to point 2 and then rose to point 3. From point 3 it subsequently fell to point 4. Point 3 is at a higher level than point 1. Also, the decline to point 4 is not as low as the previous decline to point 2. Thus, according to the DJTA, the market is still bullish. What is an investor supposed to do in a situation where the averages are giving conflicting signals? Dow's rule in a situation such as this was that *a trend will continue until its reversal has been definitely signaled*. Thus, given that the market had been bullish before all these conflicting signals appeared, Dow followers would consider it likely that the market had remained bullish through this time period. Nothing about the future can be said from these trends. In the next period the market may become bearish, but it is too early to say this when the market is at point *D*. The upshot of this example is that looking at only one index may have prompted us to prematurely declare the end of a primary trend when it in fact may not have ended. If, on the other hand, the two averages were moving in the same direction, they would be confirming each other, and any conclusion we draw about the market would be more certain.

Let's now turn to another hypothetical market scenario, shown in Figure 5-4, to better understand Dow's principle of confirmation. The figure shows weekly movements in the DJIA and DJTA. Originally, the market is bullish, with both the averages rising and DJTA's rise being weaker. At point *A* the DJIA's rally ends, and from there it reverses down to *B*. Notice that the DJTA is not tracking this. It moves up to point *B*, although it is a barely discernible upward move. This market appears reasonably sanguine about the future prospects of the economy. The fall in the DJIA probably is caused by investor profit taking. The DJIA begins a rally at *B*, and this strong rally to *C* beats the previous peak attained by the bull market. Surprisingly, the DJTA does not accompany this rally but remains rather subdued. In fact, it loses a bit of ground. By the looks of it, the DJTA is having trouble crossing level *B*. And now we are in a situation where the two averages do not conform. Is a change in the bullish market in the offing, or will it continue with the DJTA getting its act together?

From point *C*, the DJIA loses ground and falls to *D*, which is at a lower level than the point reached in the previous decline. The DJTA also has been turning steadily downward during this time. A bearish market appears likely. The averages do conform now, after all. But let's look at

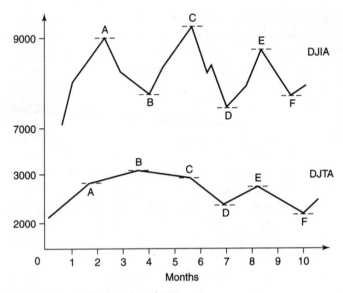

Figure 5-4 Weekly movements in the DJIA and DJTA.

another period to be sure of the market trend. From *D* the DJIA rallies to *E* but fails to beat the previous rally. The DJTA tracks this and moves from *D* to *E*, but it fails to beat its previous peak. In the next downturn, both averages fall to lower levels than before. Now a bearish trend definitely has emerged in the market. According to the Dow theory, it is a necessary condition for the averages to confirm each other for us to be able to say anything clear about the market trend. If they do not confirm each other, then the market is in *temporary disequilibrium.* This is likely to be corrected in the near future.

VOLUME FOLLOWS THE PRIMARY TREND

Technical analysis is the practice of looking at stock prices and volume concurrently to predict future price movements. It is thus not surprising that the Dow theory would have something to say about the significance of trading volume in the market. Changes in volume tell investors about the supply and demand conditions in the market. If a stock's price increases, we know that there is stronger demand for it, and if it goes down, we know that supply is stronger. However, we cannot tell by looking only at price how strong the forces of demand and supply are. For this we need to look at volume. According to the Dow theory, the trading volume accompanying price change is supposed to demonstrate the strength or weakness of a bullish or bearish primary trend. If a stock's price increases by 1 point on a trade of 5000 shares, this implies demand for the stock. However, if its price increases by 1 point and 20,000 shares are traded, this would imply much stronger demand. This also would suggest that the upward pressure on price is stronger. The stronger the trading volume associated with a bullish market, the stronger the bullish trend would be. Conversely, if a stock's price is falling on heavy trading, this would imply strong desire on the part of investors to sell. The bearish trend would be strong then.

A typically bullish trend would be characterized by heavy trading during the rallies and relatively moderate trading during the corrections. A typically bearish trend, on the other hand, would have high trading during the downturns and low trading during the reversals. The way to predict the end of a bullish trend is to see if trading volume is going down during subsequent rallies. If rallies are accompanied by weaker trading than in previous rallies, we know that while some investors are bullish, most are being cautious. This would signal that the bullish trend is weakening. If there is a significant weakening in trading during rallies, we can predict that a change in the trend is imminent. A bearish trend, on the other hand, would get weaker with a reduction in selling by traders, and a significant decline in trading could signal the end of the trend.

What we have discussed about the significance of volume here is applicable to both individual stocks and the market as a whole. Thus one could look at the DJIA and see price changes and associated trading levels to judge the nature of the market trend. Many technicians use a ratio of upside versus downside volume to gauge the short-term momentum of the stock market as a whole. This is a daily index that calculates the trading volume of stocks whose values increased divided by stocks whose values declined in the entire market. Usually this value ranges between 0.5 and 2. The rule of thumb technical analysts tend to follow is that a value of 0.7 or lower suggests that people have bought way too many stocks, i.e., the market is *overbought*, and they will start selling, which will begin a bearish trend. A value of 1.5 or above suggests that investors have sold too many stocks given the market fundamentals, or that the market is *oversold*. In this situation, investors are likely to start buying, which will start a bullish trend.

What we must remember is that the main indicator of the market trend is, of course, the movement in price. If there is significant trading in the market but negligible change in price, we cannot say much about the market trend. Volume only helps us read price signals better.

OTHER CONCEPTS AND SOME CONCLUDING THOUGHTS

Charles Dow had some thoughts on phenomena such as line formation, double tops, and double bottoms. These concepts were touched on in previous chapters. A *line formation* in Dow theory is a sideways movement in the market averages. Dow theorists would contend that such movement could last up to a few weeks and that the averages would tend to fluctuate within 5 percent of their mean value. This is a period when buying and selling pressures are roughly equivalent, and as a result the market price does not jump up or down much. This would have to change sooner or later as demand and supply conditions changed. If the averages were to make a breakout upward through the resistance level, Dow theorists would argue that this is signal that a bullish trend is about to begin. If the averages were to make a breakout downward through the support level, they would predict a bullish trend.

Dow viewed *double tops* and *double bottoms* as phenomena where the averages are failing to attain new highs or falling below a certain point. This inability to break thresholds is a sign that the primary trend of the market is likely to be changing.

Dow looked only at closing prices for his analysis. He felt that even though prices fluctuate a lot during a day, the price investors ought to use to compare one day with another is the closing price. There are only so many prices one can use as a benchmark for comparison, and it is best to settle on the day-end price, when all the dust of the day has settled.

Dow theory is not without its detractors. One criticism is that it very often misses the beginnings and ends of bullish or bearish trends. Critics argue that investors using the Dow theory to judge when to enter or leave the market are usually off the mark by around 20 percent and therefore lose out on significant profit opportunities. Dow theory enthusiasts defend their position by saying that it is never possible to predict every trend accurately, and even if investors miss the exact beginning or end of a trend, they are still assured handsome returns if they can figure out bullish and bearish trends soon enough. To believers in the Dow methodology, there are no better ways to determine market trends than using Dow concepts. In his book *Technical Analysis of the Financial Markets,* John Murphy shows figures indicating that between 1920 and 1975, using concepts of the Dow theory helped capture correctly 68 percent of the moves in the DJIA and 67 percent of the S&P500 moves.

The Dow theory is one of the earliest manifestations of technical analysis. It was developed originally to use market averages to predict the overall health of business in the economy. It quickly developed into a technical tool for predicting market trends and price movements and is still used today to make forecasts of the market. The Dow theory is more concerned with the aggregate market than with individual price movements. For predicting individual price movements, the technician already has a string of tools available. For aggregate market analysis, however, the Dow theory is the workhorse. And if stocks generally tend to move in the same direction, one can extrapolate information about individual stocks from aggregate market behavior. In addition, an investor may choose to use any other "broader" market index, such as the S&P500 instead of the DJIA, and still use Dow concepts to predict the nature of trends in the market.

6

MOVING AVERAGES, MOMENTUM, AND MARKET SWINGS

This chapter takes a closer look at moving averages, momentum, and market sentiment indicators, as well as other ways to detect market swings. To begin with, we look at the issue of moving averages, which we touched on in previous chapters and generally are related to the fundamental ideas behind technical analysis.

MOVING AVERAGES

We briefly looked at moving averages in Chapter 5. Sometimes a moving average is also referred to as an *ordinary moving average* or a *simple moving average*. It is calculated by taking the last *n* closing prices, adding them up, and then dividing by *n*. The averaging process is the same as taking the average grade of students in a class or the batting average of a baseball player. The difference is that here, instead of calculating the average grade of n students, you calculate the average price over the last n days. There are several arguments in favor of taking a moving average of stocks.

Recall that when we think of how stock prices progress, we think of the general direction of a stock price movement as following both a primary trend in the long run and also short-term secondary trends. The short-term trends fluctuate around the primary trend, moving prices up and down erratically in short bursts. For example, in a bull market, the general movement of a stock price may be increasing, but these short-term trends may be present throughout the increase, moving prices up and down. Suppose that we believe that a certain stock is following an upward trend but that there are these noisy short-term trends fluctuating around this upward market trend. An investor in this case may be holding a long position in this stock and would like to know when the upward trend will discontinue so that he or she can liquidate the position close to the market top. Whenever the stock begins to move down, the investor must consider whether this downward movement means that the market has reached its top and will begin to decline or if it is just a temporary departure from an ongoing trend. These temporary departures are sometimes called *whipsaws*. Whipsaws are temporary departures from the trend; they are quick movements away and then back to the primary trend.

The problem for investors is to detect when a departure from the primary trend is a true reversal and when it is a whipsaw. A moving average helps technicians sort out whipsaw movements from true reversals in the primary trend. To get an idea of how a moving average does this, consider the following example regarding a market with an upward trend. In such a trend, prices are generally increasing, so we would expect that without any whipsaws, the price today would be higher than the price yesterday. Suppose that we denote time with the subscript t and prices with the letter p so that the price today is p_t and the price yesterday is p_{t-1} because it is a day before. Then in an upward-trending market we would expect that the difference between p_t and p_{t-1} (which we can call x_t) is positive:

$$p_t - p_{t-1} = x_t > 0 \qquad (6.1)$$

That is, if we are in a rising market, then the price today is higher than the price yesterday, and the increase in prices is given by x_t. This is, of course, in a situation where there are no whipsaws, and the market is increasing smoothly. Obviously, we cannot expect the market to increase quite so smoothly in real life because then everyone would buy, wait for the price to rise, and sell (no one would be interested in selling at the beginning of the upward market trend or buying at the end). In real life, the price will not be increasing smoothly and then suddenly stop and fall smoothly. It will increase and fall back and be subject to endless deviations, irregular movements, and whipsaws. If the market in general is increasing, however, we would expect that, on average, $x_t > 0$ because prices do go higher in an upward market. This is exactly what the moving average looks for.

$$p_t - p_{t-1} = x_t + \varepsilon_t \tag{6.2}$$

In Equation (6.2) we are saying that the difference between today's price and yesterday's price is the average increase and some random number ε_t. It is important to realize that the random number ε_t can be negative or positive. For this reason, if ε_t is a negative number, such as –2, and x_t is a positive number, such as 1.2, then the change in prices will be negative, because the $x_t + \varepsilon_t$ will equal –0.8. Hence, in this example, prices will fall by 0.8 rather than increase by 1.2. Because prices fall 0.8, some investors may believe that the trend is now downward, but it is not. The moving average (MA) alleviates this problem by averaging out the random errors represented by ε_t. For example, a 4-day moving average would look like this:

$$\frac{1}{4} \times (p_t + p_{t-1} + p_{t-2} + p_{t-3}) = \frac{1}{4} \times [(p_{t-1} + x_t + \varepsilon_t) \tag{6.3}$$
$$+ (p_{t-2} + x_{t-1} + \varepsilon_{t-1}) + (p_{t-3} + x_{t-2} + \varepsilon_{t-2}) + (p_{t-4} + x_{t-3} + \varepsilon_{t-3})]$$

Note here that all we are saying is that $p_t = p_{t-1} + x_t + \varepsilon_t$, which is the same as Equation (6.2). Then we add these up and get the right-hand side of Equation (6.3). If we divide, we get

$$MA = \frac{1}{4} \times (p_t + p_{t-1} + p_{t-2} + p_{t-3}) = \frac{1}{4}$$
$$\times (p_{t-1} + p_{t-2} + p_{t-3} + p_{t-4})] + \frac{1}{4} \tag{6.4}$$
$$\times (x_t + x_{t-1} + x_{t-2} + x_{t-3}) + \frac{1}{4}$$
$$\times \{\varepsilon_t + \varepsilon_{t-1} + \varepsilon_{t-2} + \varepsilon_{t-3}\}$$

Hence Equation (6.4) tells us that a moving average is the average of the prices plus the average of the increases plus the average of the random digressions. Now the important point here is that if the digressions represented by ε_t are random and they are both positive and negative, when we take an average, we should get zero. This is the same as taking a coin and flipping it, and if it lands on heads, we write down 1, and if it lands on tails, we write down −1. If we repeat this 1 million times and take an average of the 1s and −1s that we write down, we should get a number very close to zero. The point here is that the average of the terms in the braces (i.e., { }) should be close to zero. Hence the moving average becomes the sum of the average price over the last 4 days plus the average of the increase over the last 4 days plus a term that should be close to zero. By making the term in the braces close to zero, we are eliminating the whipsaws. We average them out and observe only the average growth in prices, given by the x's, or the terms in the parentheses. If we think that the market is increasing, then these growth rates should be positive, so the average price is increasing. The value of the moving averages is to average out the random errors so that investors can see the average growth rate in prices more clearly. Examples of moving averages can illustrate the value of this in interpreting charts.

Figure 6-1 presents an example of a 10-day moving average. The stock price normally used for calculating a moving average is the closing price, which is plotted on the chart alongside the moving average. We can observe that the moving-average line is much smoother and less irregular and broken in its general movement upward. As the price of this stock moves up in this market, it whipsaws back and forth. The moving average generally does not jump around as much and hence gives the technician a smoother view of the underlying trend and price swings. Notice the two arrows. An investor viewing this chart just after 10/19 roughly sees the chart up to where the first arrow is located. After this, the investor sees the market increase, level off, and begin to decline. At the second arrow the technician erroneously may consider that the market is in decline. By observing the moving average, however, the technician can establish a criterion by which to judge whether the trend has reversed its direction or not.

The criterion that most traders use for deciding whether a reversal has occurred in the trend involves whether the moving average has been penetrated by the current stock price. For example, the arrow on the right in Figure 6-1 shows the stock price going lower than the moving average. This situation would draw the attention of technicians as a possible sell signal. That is, when traders see the current price fall below the moving average,

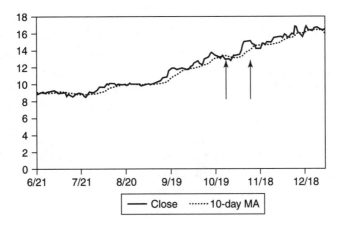

Figure 6-1 Closing price and 10-day moving average.

they consider it to be a bearish signal. This makes sense because if the stock price falls below its average, it is showing a strong declining component. Recall that the price can be thought of as $p_t = p_{t-1} + x_t + \varepsilon_t$. Thus today's price is yesterday's price plus the amount that the yesterday's price should have changed on the basis of the current trend (this is x_t) plus a random number (this is ε_t). Now recall that the moving average alleviates the effect of the randomness in prices (i.e., ε_t). When today's price falls below the average, we are either observing a change in x_t or a very large ε_t. Thus, when this occurs, technicians are aware that something unusual is happening. What they do is wait to see if the price continues downward or returns to the moving-average line. If it does not return quickly, technicians sell. If it does, they consider it a whipsaw and ignore it. Of course, at the same time they are watching for the behavior of prices in relation to their moving averages, they complement these signals with other market signals to verify which way the stock should move.

The idea behind the use of moving averages is that they behave like trend lines that follow the movement of a stock. They are a more sophisticated sort of trend line that need not restrict itself to being a straight line but rather can be curved and turn up or down, always depending on what the market is doing. Hence a penetration of the moving-average line is similar to a penetration of a trend line. Along these same lines, it is generally viewed as a more significant market move if a moving-average line that has not been penetrated for a long time or has been tested several times by the market is finally penetrated.

Penetrations of the moving-average line are sometimes called *crossovers*. When a crossover occurs and the stock price does not revert back to the moving-average line, this is a sign that the trend has suffered a reversal. The stock price will stay below the moving average, and the average stops increasing, turns around, and begins falling (assuming that the original trend was an upward market, of course). This makes sense because you begin adding to the average of prices new lower prices every day. Hence, if the market was in an upward trend, x_t is assumed to be positive, which just means that the prices usually go higher day after day. If the market now has a downward trend, x_t becomes negative day after day, and prices go lower each day than the preceding day. As a result, the price will stay below the moving-average line on downward-trending markets because each price added to the average is lower than all the previous prices. Similarly, in an upward market, prices should remain above the moving-average line because each new price added to the average should be higher than the previous prices.

The simplest rules that technicians use to discriminate a whipsaw versus a true change in the primary trend are usually based on two categories. The first is time, and the second is percentage change in price. The rules based on percentage change in price tell the technician that if the price crosses over the moving-average line and then keeps going a certain percentage, it is not a whipsaw. Usually the stock price will have to penetrate the moving average and move away from it a distance of at least 5 percent of the price. For example, the technician will use a rule that if the price falls 10 percent below the moving average, it probably is not a whipsaw. This is the sort of rule of thumb that a technician will use to decide that the penetration of the moving-average line signals a trend reversal. The actual percentage that the technician uses is based on how much risk he or she is willing to assume and how volatile the stock is. For example, a rule of 10 percent would be useful for a stock price for which a whipsaw does not represent a movement bigger than 10 percent. The idea is that if the stock moves beyond the percentage allowed by the technician, the technician buys or sells (depending on what the signal is). The technician will incur transaction costs in buying or selling, and if the technician is betting that the price will fall, for example, and it whipsaws, will have the stock move against him or her, so will incur double the mistake.

The other rule used to determine if a crossover is a simple whipsaw or an important trend reversal is even easier to figure out than a percentage change. This rule involves how much time or how many trading periods the price spends on the other side of the moving-average line. If the market begins as an ascending market, for example, the price usually should be above its moving-average line. If it moves below the moving average, then this signals a potential reversal because prices will be decreasing, which is obviously not consistent with an upward trend. The price can stay below the average for a few periods, but after a while, technicians will begin to suspect that the price has moved below the average for longer than a whipsaw and that the market is turning. Thus technicians usually develop a rule of thumb based on time spent on the opposite side of the prevailing trend. One rule is that if a price stays on the other side of the moving-average line for the same number of periods as the number of periods used to calculate the moving average, the market has begun a reversal. Thus, using this rule, for example, if we are employing a 10-day moving average in an upward-trending market and the price spends 10 days below the moving-average line, we start to believe that the market has turned downward.

Which price to use in calculating the moving average is a question of some importance for traders and technicians. For example, is the most useful moving average based on opening prices, closing prices, daily highs, or daily lows? The answer for most technicians is to go with the most stable price available that corresponds to the time period in question. For example, if a technician is calculating a moving average based on daily data, the data selected will be the representation of the price on the market for each day. The choice of most technicians in the case of daily-data moving averages is to use the daily closing price because this price best represents the market's expectation of what the long-term value of the assets is. We interpret the closing price in this way because it is that price which determines from the market the expectations of the participants when they know that they have to hold their positions overnight. Thus the closing price holds the market consensus of what the value is worth for the longest period available in daily data, which is the overnight period. Similarly, most technicians, when working with a moving average based on weekly data, use the Friday closing price in their averaging. This price also represents the market consensus on what the long-term value of the asset is for the longest period available in weekly data, which is the weekend. Thus traders going home for the weekend know that their positions have to hold at the closing price no matter what kind of news or developments occur while the markets are closed. Were the markets to open during the weekend, investors could adjust their portfolios in response to developments. Since the markets do not open, investors must hold their positions and absorb this risk. The closing price captures these expectations.

TIME SPAN AND MOVING AVERAGES

Here we are pursuing an unseen motion in prices. That is, the trend is some kind of moving thing, something unseen that we detect with moving averages. It is not like finding a building in a city; it is like finding a person who will not sit still in the same place. As a result, we have two problems with trying to detect the trend. The first is whether we are sure that we know where it is, and the second is whether we can be sure of where it is going. One of the most fundamental ideas in physics is the principle that the more we know about a particle's location, the less we know about its momentum, and vice versa. Here we face exactly the same problem. The first problem has to do with making sure that we are actually seeing the true market trend and not some temporary market aberration. The second problem is that even if we think that we know where the trend was yesterday, as long as markets are open and people are trading stocks, the potential for the trend to have completely reversed from where we thought it was is a distinct possibility. That is, there is an ever-present risk that the market may shift and our past assessments of the market may become obsolete in a very short period of time. The more we know about where the trend is by looking at past data, the less we have a feel for how it is moving by looking at the most recent data coming in.

Moving averages, as we saw, help alleviate the first problem, the problem of short-run fluctuations that are not representative of the primary trend in the market. The moving average helps us know exactly where the trend is right now. The problem is that the more precise we are about the overall trend, the less precise we are about where it is going. That is, by using a moving average, we have added problems to figuring out in which direction the stock is moving; the moving average brings in an additional nuisance. This nuisance comes in because basing moving averages on past data implies that the technician is ignoring some of the most recent price movements in favor of past movements. The good news about moving averages is that we average out the noisy, erratic, short-run movements by including past stock prices, and this is good, because we avoid whipsaws. The bad news is that we average out the true early movements of a change in the trend. The ability to detect a change in the trend early in the movement could mean the difference between a profit and a loss. For example, if every day for the last 10 weeks the market has been in decline and I have a moving average, then it will show a downward trend. Suppose that today is the first day of the turn in this trend, and prices increase. If I only look at the trend, it will take some time before the average price is increasing. In all this time, I am losing profit opportunities by not buying and taking the long position in an increasing market.

This tradeoff is most acute in longer moving averages. If we take a 10-day moving average, it will show some variability. If we make it a 30-day moving average, it will show almost no daily trading variability. Figure 6-2 shows an example of a stock in which the 30-day moving average is very smooth, so the trader avoids many unnecessary whipsaws, but he or she also avoids getting in early on some of the larger movements of the stock. Notice that the first arrow on the left shows where the 10-day moving average would have signaled a potential buying opportunity for the technician. The second higher arrow, which is on the right, shows where the technician using the same 10-day moving average would have sold. Clearly, these entry and exit points would not have been apparent to the technician using the 30-day moving average. In the best-case scenario, the technician using the 30-day moving average would have bought at a higher price and sold at a lower price and thus would have missed out on some of the profit opportunities for this movement. Notice, however, that the third arrow, which is the furthest to the right, shows a sequence of whipsaws that may affect the technician using the 10-day moving average but not the one using the 30-day moving average.

Thus the technician faces a tradeoff inherent in a longer time span of the moving average: a lower risk of whipsaws but also a lower profit because of arriving too late to market reversals and selling too late as well.

The first thing a technician will do to alleviate this problem is to not center the moving average. *Centering* a moving average means to enter the number of the average on the day in the middle of the averaging period. That is, if we take a 10-day moving average, we enter that number on the fifth day on the price charts. The reasoning behind centering is that if we are taking an average of the market based on the movement of prices over 10 days, true average movement over the 10 days is correct

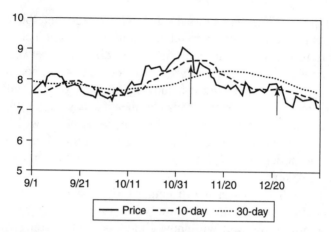

Figure 6-2 Closing price, 10-day moving average, and 30-day moving average. Note that the 30-day moving average is the smoothest line; it displays much less short-run fluctuation.

for the fifth day. It is on the fifth day that the average gives the most accurate picture of the trend. The problem is that centering makes the technician wait even longer to observe a reversal than the normal moving average. Thus it is not commonly done when technicians are using moving averages for this purpose.

The next technique used to alleviate the problem of learning about reversals when it is already too late is to *shift the moving average forward*. This is the opposite of centering the moving average, which shifts the number back. An example will illustrate this easy idea (Figure 6-3). Suppose that we have a 10-day moving average. We could have, for example, on May 20 the average of the last 10 business days and on May 21 the preceding 10 business days (including May 20), and so on. If we center the moving average, the entry for May 20 would be from May 16 to May 25 (here we are ignoring weekends and holidays for purposes of exposition). If we project the moving average forward, we let May 20 be the average of the prices from May 6 to May 15, for example. The point is that the price on May 20 does not affect the moving average of May 20. When we advance the moving average in the calendar, or project it forward, we do not allow today's stock price to affect today's moving average.

Notice in Figure 6-3 that the 10-day moving average is projected forward 7 days. Also depicted is the normal 10-day moving average, which appears on the chart as the entry for the tenth day (i.e., today's

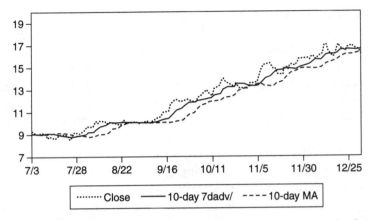

Figure 6-3 This is a 10-day, 7-day advanced moving average. This means that the value for today in the moving average is projected forward 7 business days. Consequently, on the chart, the moving-average entry for each day is the same as the 10-day moving average without forward projection but from 7 days prior (which is also depicted).

10-day average is today's price averaged with the price from the previous 9 days; the 7-day projection implies that today's moving average is the price from 7 days ago averaged with the 9 days previous to it). Note the 7-day projection line seems to imitate the normal moving average. They are the same line, just drawn starting at different dates. This difference is important for technicians, however. Note that the projection moves away from the stock price and allows for the whipsaws to decrease.

WEIGHTED MOVING AVERAGES

Another technique used to help improve the agility of moving averages in detecting market swings and changes in the underlying market trend is *weighted moving averages*. These are averages where the most recent observations are made to matter more than the rest. That is, the most recently observed stock prices are counted more than the stock prices that were observed further in the past. The further back in time a stock price was observed, the less it counts in the weighted moving average. The idea is that the moving average should reflect the more recent data more than it reflects data that are there solely for the purpose of averaging out errors but not for adding any sort of information about where the market is heading. This is similar to saying that when we think about where the market is heading, we look to the Dow Jones Industrial Average (DJIA) because it comprises the largest and most important companies in the United States. These companies will reflect more quickly and accurately the general sentiments of the market than will some unknown small-cap stock. Similarly, the most recent data have the most recent innovations in the mood of the market and the determinants of the underlying market trend embedded in them. Thus such data would be of more use in predicting where tomorrow's price will be than will a price from 10 days ago.

To construct a weighted moving average (WMA), instead of adding n numbers together and then dividing by n, we multiply each number by a separate fraction. Suppose, for example, that we were doing a 4-day moving average. For an ordinary moving average, we just add the price of the last 4 days and divide by 4, as in Equation (6.1). For a weighted moving average, we want the most recent days to count more than the others. As a result, if today is p_t, yesterday is p_{t-1}, and so on, we may add the following:

$$\text{WMA} = (\tfrac{1}{15}) \times p_{t-3} + (\tfrac{2}{15}) \times p_{t-2} + (\tfrac{4}{15}) \times p_{t-1} + (\tfrac{8}{15}) \times p_t \quad (6.5)$$

In Equation (6.5) we see an example of a weighted moving average. The fractions in parentheses next to the price for each day are called the *weights*. Notice that the price today (time t) is counted eight times more than the price 3 days ago (time $t - 3$). It is important to stress that the weights used in Equation (6.5) are completely arbitrary and that each technician adjusts the moving average to where he or she feels it is best. One common rule of thumb used to develop a set of weights is to sum the numbers in the number of lags. For example, in Equation (6.5) we are using a 4-day moving average. Thus we would sum $1 + 2 + 3 + 4$, one for each day. The sum of these is 10. Then we would just divide by 10, and use the numbers in the sum divided by 10 as weights. In this case, Equation (6.5) would become

$$\text{WMA} = (\tfrac{1}{10}) \times p_{t-3} + (\tfrac{2}{10}) \times p_{t-2} + (\tfrac{3}{10}) \times p_{t-1} + (\tfrac{4}{10}) \times p_t \quad (6.6)$$

It is important to note that because moving averages respond more quickly and in a different way to a change in the price, a crossover is not the criterion used by technicians to detect a reversal in the underlying primary market trend. For example, in Figure 6-4a we have taken an

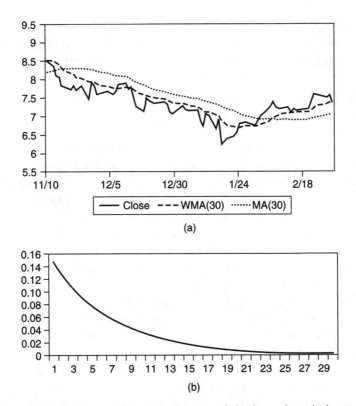

Figure 6-4 (*a*) A weighted moving average (WMA). It was calculated as a damped Fibonacci coefficient moving average, where the coefficients are fractions with the furthest two lags having a numerator of unity and each subsequent lag having a numerator equal to the previous numerator plus 20 percent of the twice-previous numerator. The denominator is the sum of all the numerators for all coefficients. (*b*) A graph of the weighted coefficients. Notice that the farther back in time the lags go, the less they are weighted. The ordinary moving average is a straight average of the past 30 prices.

ordinary 30-day moving average (MA) and a weighted moving average (WMA). Ordinary moving averages with this many lags generally are very smooth and unresponsive lines because of the intense averaging that occurs with 30 price lags. Yet in the figure we see that the weighted moving average is not at all like the regular moving average. As a result, technicians looking at crossovers look beyond for changes in the direction of a moving average as a sign of a change in the underlying trend. They also try different kinds of weights, depending on how much sensitivity they desire for the most recent prices. In the bottom panel of Figure

6-4*b* we can see a depiction of the coefficients. Notice that the farther back in time the lags go, the less they are weighted, and furthermore, the weights decline quickly, which gives the line the round, curvy shape.

MOVING AVERAGES AND SIDEWAYS-TRENDING MARKETS

Recall that the idea behind a moving average is to average out the random numbers that jump around the basic trend. If the trend is increasing, then the market will show a generally upward-sloping but jarring and erratic line. The moving average in this case should be a smoothly increasing line because the randomness will average out to zero. The analogous situation holds for the case of a downward-trending market. The point to keep in mind here is that the moving average works to average out to zero the randomness in stock prices so that the primary trend can be revealed. The problem is that sometimes the primary trend is at a point that is neither increasing nor decreasing. At this point, the market is in a *sideways trend*. If we go back to Equation (6.1), a sideways market is like having x_t always come up as zero. Thus the only thing the averaging of prices does is to eliminate the randomness in ε_t without revealing an upward or downward movement. This creates a problem for technicians using moving averages. They may expect the market to show an upward or downward trend, but if the trend is sideways, they will be looking for something that is not there. This is why it is important to keep an open mind when looking at technical indicators; they can be subject to the biases of the technician, and without objectivity, they can cause more harm than good. In this case, a technician who is looking for an upward trend may buy at every crossover. If the market is in a sideways trend, every crossover will be a whipsaw, however. As a result, the technician who does not recognize the sideways trend will be forced to absorb losses.

Sideways trends are one of the biggest potential problems that technicians face when using moving averages. In response to this situation, some technicians rely on triggering mechanisms to initiate a moving average. What this means is that they do not bother looking at a moving average unless certain red flags go up. For example, a technician may think that the market is not in a strong enough upward or downward trend but more in a sideways trend. As a result, the technician may not rely on a moving average for signs of a breakout initially. Instead, the technician may look for certain signals in the market that tell him or her when to start looking at a moving average. These signals serve to warn the technician that the market may be ready to break out of the sideways trend. Since moving averages are of little use in a sideways market, these signals serve to indicate when the use of moving averages becomes appropriate. One such red flag is that a price goes higher than a certain number of days' high price. For example, the technician will set a window of 6 days and not use a moving average unless the closing price goes higher than all the highs of the past 6 days. As a result, the price going higher signals that the market may be breaking out, or testing the resistance of the sideways market. Similarly, the technician may not look at moving averages unless the price goes lower than the lows of the past 6 days. These sorts of signals then would imply that the technician looks at moving averages only when the price begins to move more broadly. These broader movements probably would not be too common in sideways markets, and consequently, this technique would reduce the whipsaw costs of using a moving average in a sideways market. Adjustments to the size of the window commonly are made on the basis of the volatility of the stock and the overall market in general. If the stock is very volatile, then longer windows are used so that the level that the price should exceed is more significant.

ENVELOPES AND BOLLINGER BANDS

Envelopes and Bollinger bands are techniques closely related to the technique just discussed. The first, *envelopes,* are also sometimes referred to as *trading bands.* When a technician uses an envelope in conjunction with a moving average, he or she is drawing lines that define on either side of a moving average what is "in bounds" for the market and what is "out of bounds." That is, on the graph there are two more lines, one above the moving average line and one below the moving average line, that move exactly the same way the moving-average line moves. There are at least two easy ways to get started with envelopes. The first is to add and subtract some fixed amount to and from the moving average at each point. The second is to add and subtract some fixed percentage of the moving average to and from itself. For example, using the first method, we add 5 to and subtract 5 from the moving-average price each day, whereas with the second technique, we may add and subtract 10 percent of the moving-average price. An example of an envelope is shown in Figure 6-5.

When a price is in the "in bounds" range, it is not making a significant movement. The technician considers it highly likely that the price movements inside this range are whipsaws. If a price moves above the

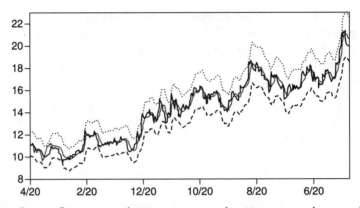

Figure 6-5 The price fluctuates around a moving average with a 10 percent envelope around it. The technician will adjust the envelope to the desired range. Here, the envelope is very wide for purposes of illustration.

upper line, the technician looks at this as evidence of a possible shift in the underlying trend. The same goes for the lower band.

Bollinger bands are closely related to envelopes. They are bands or lines drawn above and below the moving-average line just like envelopes. The difference between the two lies in the way the distance from the moving-average line to the bands is calculated. These bands, named after John Bollinger, use a very simple and well-known statistical calculation called *confidence intervals*. Economists, statisticians, and scientists in all fields use confidence intervals when they want to calculate an area around a number where they are, say, 90 percent sure that the true number lies. For example, suppose that Ford Motor Company hires an economist to calculate the number of cars projected to sell in the coming month. The economist may use models of demand for cars and so on to derive an estimate. This estimate, however, most likely will not be exactly correct. That is, the economist may tell Ford that he or she estimates that the company will sell 10,000 cars. If the company sells 10,562 cars, the economist's estimate will have been very close, but wrong. Since it is almost impossible to predict the exact number of cars sold in advance, the economist usually will report a confidence interval within which he or she expects the true number of cars sold to end up. The confidence interval is a neighborhood around which the true number should be.

In similar fashion, a Bollinger band calculates a confidence interval around the moving average, based on the variation in prices. This is much better than using a fixed percentage or a fixed number to create the band around the moving-average line because the Bollinger band takes into account the estimated variability of the stock. Instead of the technician eyeballing the data and guessing how far the price should move before it is an unusually significant movement, this technique gives you the exact size of the movement. What these bands do is look at a certain number of past days' prices and calculate how big the random movements of the prices are. If we know how big an average random movement is, we can figure out how big a random movement has to be to be bigger than 90 percent of the other erratic and unexpected price jumps. We can calculate a band that represents the area where a price can jump around and still not be bigger than 90 percent of the random movements in prices. Then, when the price moves outside this band, we are seeing a price movement larger than 90 percent of the random movement in the past 10 days, or whatever the relevant window of days is. Technicians would expect that these large movements are most likely not whipsaws because very large whipsaws are not common.

There are two points to notice about this technique. The first is that the technician must select the past number of days to use in calculating the randomness of a stock. The more days used, the more accurate is the picture of stock price randomness. The tradeoff is that past randomness may not be relevant to stock prices because they are subject to periods of high volatility followed by periods of low volatility. The second point is that this technique adjusts to the current stock price volatility (in the window considered), so the band becomes narrower during periods of low volatility and wider during periods of high volatility. This is good for the technician because it allows a more dynamic and accurate assessment of current market conditions rather than using a fixed percentage or quantity no matter what the conditions of the market are.

Figure 6-6 shows a moving average smoothing the price fluctuations and a Bollinger band around it. The band is calculated on a 10-day window, as is the moving average. Here we have set the band to 2 standard deviations from the moving average, which means that upwards of 90 percent of the volatility in prices will be contained within it. As can be observed in the figure, this band is very wide during periods of high volatility and grows narrower during periods of low volatility by construction.

When the bands grow narrower, the implication is that the volatility in prices is declining. In such a situation, the trading could be very tight

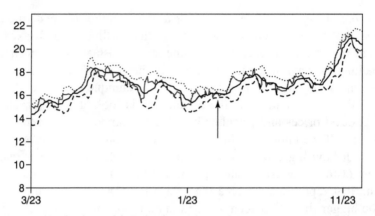

Figure 6-6 An example of a confidence band around a 10-day moving average. Here, the confidence band also bases the volatility estimates on a 10-day window. Notice that the band gets narrower as the price volatility is reduced.

as the bulls and bears battle it out in a very close contest to see who can push the price in their direction. After the dust settles, the resulting price movement can be very large because the other side of the market will be very weak from the contest. This idea is similar to the idea of pennants discussed in Chapter 4. The difference here is that the technician is not eyeballing the data to see a reduction in the volatility; the actual calculated volatility bands are declining in these markets. Thus, when this occurs, it is not uncommon to see a large and pronounced movement in the prices of stocks. An example of this phenomenon is indicated in Figure 6-6 with the arrow. Here we can see the bands coming closer together, and then a sharp increasing resulting.

A further implication that can be observed is that if the prices are on one side of the moving-average line and they push past the confidence bands on that same side, technicians interpret this as evidence that the underlying trend will continue. The reason is that with prices already on one side of the moving-average line, there is reason to believe that the primary trend indicated by the moving average is continuing. With the price exceeding the band, there is evidence to suggest that the price movement is strengthening the primary trend. If, however, the price moves to one band, it often will bounce and react by touching the opposite band. That is, large movements in the one direction often follow large movements in the opposite direction.

The calculation of a confidence band around a moving average is usually done with a spreadsheet program because it can be intensive, but it is definitely not a difficult task to accomplish. The first step is to get a moving average. This average can be weighted, or whatever the technician decides is best, because the band surrounds the moving average but does not depend on it to calculate the variability of stocks. The next step is to perform the following simple calculations:

$$\text{Upper band} = MA_t + \theta \times [(1/n)\Sigma(p_t - MA_t)^2]^{1/2} \qquad (6.7)$$

$$\text{Lower band} = MA_t - \theta \times [(1/n)\Sigma(p_t - MA_t)^2]^{1/2} \qquad (6.8)$$

Here θ represents the number of standard deviations desired by the technician. If we use 2 standard deviations, we are covering 95 percent of the variation calculated in the window of days. Inside the brackets, we divide by n, the number of days the quantity represented by the sum (the Greek letter Σ means that one adds the terms to the right of it) of the squared difference between the price on day t and the moving average on day t. Thus we get an average of the squared difference between price and moving average and then take the square root of this number.

MOMENTUM

The overall idea behind moving averages is to smooth out erratic short-run movements in the data, which means that moving averages smooth out the ε_t shocks (recall that we defined the change in prices as $p_t - p_{t-1} = x_t + \varepsilon_t$). The overall idea behind momentum is to not look so much at ε_t and focus more on x_t, which is the change in the price from one day to the next. By looking at x_t, we are looking at the component of prices that is changing due to shifts in the underlying patterns of supply and demand. That is, x_t is the component of the change in prices that is due to changes in what people believe the stock is worth in the long run, which reflects the price at which supply and demand come together in the markets. There is a general consensus among technicians that the market is driven by fear and greed. Thus momentum captures the changes in the optimism or pessimism of market participants, in addition to capturing the effects on a stock price of changes that occur outside the market, such as changes in the overall state of the economy, and so on.

When physicists talk of momentum, they are talking about the quantity of motion in an object. For example, a physicist may roughly describe the momentum of a car driving in a straight line as its mass times its velocity. In technical analysis, momentum is thought of as the general propensity of a stock price to keep moving in a given direction. That is, when looking at the momentum of a stock price, technicians try to figure out how likely it is that the stock will keep on going the way it has been going. This is a very general characterization of what the idea behind momentum is because there are many different and wide-ranging ways of measuring the momentum of a stock price or a market. When trying to measure the momentum of a stock price, technicians are trying to measure a component that is quite abstract and impalpable, which is the market sentiment regarding that stock. There is no surefire way to gauge what the market thinks and the pessimism or optimism regarding the future of a stock of all market participants. Among other reasons, such measures would have to include the potential market participants who are not holding the stock but could jump into the market in the near future. This is very difficult, but there is a consensus among technicians about how momentum changes in the cycle of a stock price.

The idea of changing momentum is like the idea of a roller coaster. The price of the stock moves up and down just like the roller coaster, and the speed of the roller coaster is the momentum. Suppose that a roller coaster is shooting down an incline in the tracks and comes to the next incline. When the roller coaster begins to climb the hill, initially it roars up the hill at a very fast pace. Then, as it approaches the top, it has slowed down considerably. When it is at the top, it is almost completely stopped (in fact, some roller coasters need help getting up the hill). The stock price momentum is the same. When the stock is beginning a rally, it shoots up with a lot of momentum. As it is reaching the top of the bull market, it has lost all its momentum. Finally, at the top, it stops and starts going down again. Now it behaves just like a roller coaster going down a hill. It begins slowly, picks up speed, and comes roaring down the track. The roller coaster is going the fastest at the bottom of the hill and will keep rolling until eventually the friction of the tracks slows it down. Stock price momentum is the same for a decline. The momentum is small at the beginning of the decline and is the largest as the decline is approaching bottom, where it slows and tapers off.

Measures of this effect on the markets are interesting because technicians do not use them to predict if a change in the trend *has* occurred but rather use them to predict if a change in the markets *will* occur. That is, a technician who sees a crossover occur in a moving-average chart may believe that a change in the market trend has occurred. When the technician sees changes occur on a momentum chart, it signals that changes in the primary trend of stocks are forthcoming, not that they have already occurred. Technicians may use market-wide measures of momentum or stock-specific measures of momentum. *Market-wide measures* are measures that take into account the activity of all the stocks in general. For example, one may look at how many stock prices increased versus how many decreased as a market-wide measure of momentum. *Stock-specific measures* are those which concentrate only on one stock. For example, one may look at the rate at which the stock price is changing over a certain window of days.

Generally speaking, technicians chart momentum indicators as curves that move around a fixed line, like a snake slithering along a banister. These are called *oscillators* because they swing back and forth, fluctuating around the fixed line. Momentum is measured in these oscillators as the movement of buying momentum as the curve pushes above the fixed line and selling momentum as the curve slides below the fixed line. As with envelopes, technicians then draw two parallel lines, one above the fixed line and one below, to mark the limits of "acceptable" buying and selling momentum. Once the oscillator crosses over these lines, the stock is said to be *overbought* or *oversold.* An example of an oscillator is given in Figure 6-7.

Here we will look at some of the most common and widely used examples of momentum, but this list is not exhaustive. There are literally dozens of momentum indicators, and technicians are all the time deciding to take a new mathematical combination of volume, highs, lows, closing or opening prices, or some market breadth statistic and invent yet another momentum indicator. The end result is that there is an overabundance of indicators out there, and there is no consensus as to which or what about any one of them makes it more successful than the others. In the horse race of which the momentum indicator is best, there is obviously no clear winner, and frankly, there is not even any one indicator that looks to be clearly ahead of the pack. Therefore, it is better to understand the basics of what they are measuring, and then select an indicator that represents your idea of where an accurate measurement of market sentiment is captured.

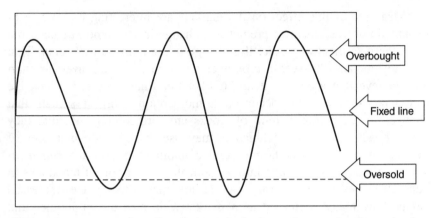

Figure 6-7 A momentum oscillator fluctuating around a fixed, or reference, value. The overbought and oversold lines are indicated. These are bearish and bullish signals of trend reversal, respectively.

Rate of Change

The *rate of change* (ROC) of a stock is given by the difference between today's price and some past price divided by the past price. That is,

$$\text{ROC} = \frac{(p_t - p_{t-k})}{p_{t-k}} \tag{6.9}$$

Notice that here we have used the letter k to indicate how far back to go. For example, if $k = 1$, the technician is calculating the rate of change from yesterday to today, whereas if $k = 10$, the technician is calculating the rate of change from 2 weeks ago to today ($k = 10$ means 10 business days ago, so that is 2 weeks). Some technicians choose to multiply Eq. (6.9) by 100 so that they can have a percent rate of change, but it makes no fundamental difference. The rate of change can never go below -1, or -100 percent, which is a result that indicates that the worst that could happen to the price today is that it becomes zero when the stock is worthless. Theoretically, the rate of change is unbounded from above, so it can go as high as it wants.

In using the rate of change, technicians draw overbought and oversold lines and look for the stock to penetrate these lines as a sign of a reversal. An important thing to keep in mind, however, is the cycle that momentum makes. Momentum is like the roller coaster. When the price is beginning to increase in a rally, momentum can be very strong. At these times it

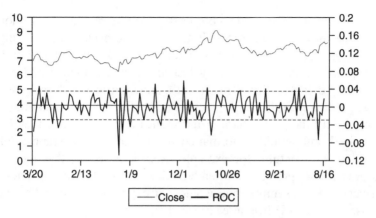

Figure 6-8 Rate of change (ROC) as a measure of momentum. This calculation used an overnight window, which gave prices very little volatility.

may appear that the stock is overbought, but because this is naturally the point at which stocks are increasing in value, technicians do not interpret this to be a sign of an end to the rally. If, however, the price is barely able to reach or remain at high levels of momentum, this in itself is a sign that advancing prices are losing momentum. Figure 6-8 illustrates rate of change as a measure of momentum.

Because the rate of change measures the increase in a stock price, it can serve as a measure of market tops and market bottoms as long as the market makes a smooth enough transition from tops to bottoms. No one can see at what price level a stock price will stop increasing and begin falling, but technicians can observe the rate at which price increases. Because they believe that prices increase a lot, then a little, then stop increasing, then decrease a little, then a lot, then a little, then stop decreasing, and so on, they believe that they can tell when the price is reaching its high. This is what momentum measures try to do. Technicians figure that when the rate of increase begins to fall, it will become zero, then negative, and then the price will soon begin to fall. Keep in mind that when the rate of change is falling, as long as it is still positive, prices are still increasing. Thus technicians observe a signal that warns them of impending reversals.

When reading the rate of change as an indicator of momentum, just as when reading any other indicator of momentum, there are certain points that one should keep in mind. Momentum works well for stocks that have smooth and easy moving cycles. If a stock shoots up one day, plummets the next day, and so on, looking at rate of change will not help predict the movement in prices. In this case, the price is not moving like a roller coaster; it is moving like a soccer ball. It may sit still and then suddenly get kicked and go very fast and then get kicked and go very fast in the other direction. This is not a situation in which momentum is a good predictor. Furthermore, technicians believe that momentum can be analyzed with the same charting techniques as prices. Thus they believe that a head and shoulders formation in the momentum graph implies a reversal in momentum, for example. Recall, however, that momentum measures are not prices, are often bounded, and have other commonsense restrictions. For example, one would not expect the price of a stock to increase too much if it is already overbought.

Advance-Decline Line

A second measure of momentum is the *advance-decline (A/D) line.* This indicator, however, looks not at one stock but rather at the market in general. It is designed to measure market strength, which means it basically looks at whether the market is in the mood to increase or decrease. The A/D line is simple and is closely related to our discussion of the Dow theory. The idea behind the A/D line is to look at how many stocks increased in value and how many decreased in value. If the number of stocks that increased is greater than the number that decreased, the A/D line moves up. The actual number of the A/D line is a running sum of this difference. For example, if 200 more stocks advanced than declined today, we add 200 to yesterday's value, and this is today's value for the A/D line. If 300 more stocks decline than advance tomorrow, we subtract 300 from today's value and call that number tomorrow's value of the A/D line. Thus everyday we just find the difference between advancing and declining issues and add that to the previous day's value.

An often cited example of how to use an A/D line is to look for a situation in which the graph of the A/D line is going in one direction and the DJIA is going in the other. For example, suppose that the DJIA is increasing, but the A/D line is falling. In this situation, the market's best and most important stocks, represented by the DJIA, are getting more expensive, but most of the stocks in the market are getting cheaper and decreasing in value. Technicians refer to this as the "generals (meaning the DJIA) are charging into battle, but the troops are not following them." Thus, just as one would expect that a bunch of army generals without any soldiers would retreat from a charge, technicians would expect that the DJIA would fall in this situation.

Closely related to the A/D line is the *A/D ratio*. Here, technicians divide the number of advancing issues by the number of declining issues. This measure has the advantage that if more stocks are traded on the New York Stock Exchange, it does not change the A/D ratio, whereas the A/D line would be affected. The A/D ratio is used in similar fashion to the rate of change. It oscillates around a fixed line, and if the value goes too high, it is taken to be a bearish sign, because the market is oversold. If the value goes too low, the opposite applies.

Relative Strength Indicator

The *relative strength index* (RSI) measures how strong stock movement is. To construct a relative strength index, a technician first chooses a window of time, say, k days (where k is the number of days in the window of time). Then he or she looks at the number of times that the stock price closed up in those k days and takes the average price change on the up days. We will call this the *up average*. The up average captures the average movement of the price on the market when the market closed up on the day in the last k days. Similarly, the technician looks at which days closed down in the last k days. He or she then takes the average price change on the down days, which we will call the *down average*. Down average captures the average closing price on days when the stock closed down on the day. The technician then forms the relative strength (RS) as

$$RS = \frac{\text{up average}}{\text{down average}} \tag{6.10}$$

$$RSI = 100 - \frac{100}{1 + RS} \tag{6.11}$$

The RSI is useful to plot alongside a price and moving-average plot. Just like the rate of change, the RSI can complete price patterns or go into the extreme zones of the charting region, signaling an overbought or oversold condition. In this case, the RSI will oscillate from 0 to 100, and usually the overbought and oversold regions are considered above 70 or below 30. There are plenty of exceptions to this rule, however; technicians adjust the lines to 75 or 80 and 25 or 20 depending on if the stock is extremely volatile. It is important to note here that all momentum indicators, and especially oscillators such as the RSI, should not be taken as sell signals or buy signals independently. All along, we have argued that technical analysis offers evidence of possible reversals and changes in primary trends. This is especially true of momentum indicators such as RSI. They should be used in conjunction with a price crossover, a price pattern, or some other signal, and then the decision to buy or sell should be made based on a preponderance of the evidence, not on one signal alone.

Note that this indicator should not be confused with the more general notion in technical analysis of relative strength. The idea of relative strength is to look at a stock, and if it is doing better than the rest of the market, this is a bullish sign for the stock. This idea is generalized to indexes of industries as well. If the technology sector is doing better than the market portfolio, this is considered bullish by technicians for that sector, for example.

Accumulation-Distribution and On-Balance Volume
The accumulation-distribution and on-balance volume indicators relate the volume of trading of a security to the market direction. The easier of the two to calculate is the *on-balance volume*. To calculate this indicator, the technician keeps a running total of daily volume, and if the market closes up on the day, adds the daily volume. If the market closes down on the day, the technician subtracts the daily volume. For the on-balance volume indicator, what technicians care about is the direction of the indicator. If it is increasing, then they believe that prices will increase. If it is decreasing, then they believe that prices will fall.

The *accumulation-distribution (A/D) indicator* is calculated with the same idea in mind, which is that usually increasing volume accompanies price increases. What this indicator does is add volume when price is rising and subtract it when price is falling. Thus, if price is rising and volume is going up, it is an *accumulation period,* and this is a bullish sign. If price is falling and volume is subtracted, it is a *distribution period,* which is a bearish sign. The calculation is as follows:

$$\text{A/D indicator} = \sum\left(\text{volume} \times \frac{(\text{close-low}) - (\text{high-close})}{(\text{high-low})}\right) \quad (6.12)$$

Notice that more volume will be added the closer the closing price is to the high price and, consequently, the further away it is from the low. In the opposite situation, more volume will be subtracted the further the closing price is from the high price.

Moving Average Convergence-Divergence

Moving Average Convergence-Divergence (MACD) is an indicator of momentum that looks to the differences in time spans of moving averages as a sign of market momentum. There are two ways to calculate MACD. The most accepted way is to take a moving average with a shorter time span and subtract a moving average with a longer time span. Some technicians take the ratio of two moving averages, however. MACD, like all the other oscillators, has the usual signals for the technician, which are a crossover of the signal line, an increase or decrease into the overbought or oversold zones, or a divergence from the market price.

Arms Index

This momentum indicator is a composite of two commonly used ratios. To calculate the *Arms index,* technicians first calculate the A/D ratio and then the upside-downside ratio. Then the Arms index is the A/D ratio divided by the upside-downside ratio.

$$\text{A/D ratio} = \frac{\text{advancing issues}}{\text{declining issues}} \tag{6.13}$$

$$\text{Upside-downside ratio} = \frac{\text{advancing volume}}{\text{declining volume}} \tag{6.14}$$

$$\text{Arms index} = \frac{\text{A/D ratio}}{\text{upside-downside ratio}} \tag{6.15}$$

In looking at the Arms index, note that the numerator [the numerator is the number on the top of the fraction; e.g., in the fraction (%), a is the numerator, and b is the denominator] captures the proportion of advancing to declining issues; we can think of it as how outnumbered declining issues are in relation to advancing issues. The larger the A/D ratio, the more outnumbered declining issues are to advancing issues. Similarly, the denominator captures how outnumbered declining volume is relative to advancing volume. The bigger the denominator, the more advancing volume is outnumbering declining volume. Thus, if the Arms index falls below 1.0, we are saying that advancing volume is outnumbering declining volume more than advancing stocks are outnumbering declining stocks. This is a bullish signal. In the opposite situation, if the Arms index increases above 1.0, advancing stocks are outnumbering declining stocks by more than advancing volume is outnumbering declining volume. This is a bearish signal. Generally, the Arms index is plotted as an oscillator, and overbought or oversold lines are used to signal potential buying or selling opportunities. As always, these signals should be complemented with analysis of price and volume for crossovers, pattern completions, and other technical indicators of trend reversals.

In this chapter we have seen two powerful tools used by technicians. The moving average is a tool in and of itself for the technician to use, as well as a way of smoothing out other signals that technicians use, such as momentum indicators. Furthermore, we have seen momentum indicators that can be used independently, or some technicians even like to find the momentum of moving averages. There are vast numbers of these indicators in existence, but what is of value for traders is not looking at dozens of numbers but rather finding a few summary statistics that give a sense of what is happening in the market with a stock or index. In the use of these indicators, each trader selects and develops a style and comfort level with a few particular indicators that he or she may have a preference for or become familiar with. Technicians, however, constantly update their skills, stay on top of new techniques and indicators, and adjust their warning levels, e.g., their overbought or oversold lines, to new market conditions and to each stock's particular features.

In the next chapter we discuss the Elliott wave theory, which essentially builds on Dow's work on the aggregate stock market. Whereas Dow spoke of trends and of phases within trends, Elliott wave theory argues that the stock market moves in wavelike motions, each wave being part of a larger wave and each wave containing smaller wave movements within it. These waves exhibit recurring patterns, and by analyzing them, one can get a sense of the waves that are to come. We thus come back to the recurring theme of technical analysis: Future movements in the stock market can be predicted from the past.

7

ELLIOTT WAVE THEORY

In Chapter 5 we discussed the Dow theory. The Elliott wave theory is closely linked to the ideas of Dow theory. Its founder, Ralph Nelson Elliott, intended it to be an extension of Dow concepts concerning market trends. As in the Dow theory, Elliott also used the Dow Jones Industrial Average (DJIA) as his basis for studying the entire stock market.

Elliott was an accountant and business consultant whose significant work, "The Wave Principle," appeared in 1938. Charles Collins, the editor of a weekly investment bulletin, assisted Elliott and was instrumental in the publication of this work. Elliott's other important work, *Nature's Law—The Secret of the Universe,* appeared in 1946, two years before his death. His ideas were popularized to a great extent by Hamilton Bolton, who published the annual journal entitled, *Bank Credit Analyst.* In 1953,

Bolton wrote an article on Elliott wave theory's applicability to the U.S. stock market. He continued to publish assessments of the U.S. stock market using this theory in the annual supplements to his journal. Subsequently, a lot of literature has developed refining and clarifying Elliott's ideas and concepts. Most notable among them is A. J. Frost and Robert Prechter's *Elliott Wave Principle: Key to Market Behavior*, which was published in 1978. A lot of the discussion in this chapter draws from this very thorough and influential book.

Elliott believed that group or social activities follow certain identifiable patterns. He believed that human actions have a "rhythmic bias" and thus can be predicted with a reasonable degree of certainty. According to him, this held true for all social, economic, and political phenomena. It also held for stock market fluctuations. To him, this was only natural, since the stock market was made up of vibrant public participation and was essentially a psychological phenomenon. If human actions demonstrated certain patterns, so should stock market movements. Human beings demonstrate their idiosyncrasies every so often, and such idiosyncrasies have a habit of recurring over time. In Chapter 5 we mentioned the occurrence of "mob behavior" in the stock market. Mob behavior is not really rational, but it seems to recur in stock markets when panic selling by investors causes the market to plunge well below its intrinsic value. What we get out of this example is that if all individuals were thinking rationally, they would not be selling and sending the market plunging to a level below its intrinsic value, but individuals do so anyway. Thus it might be safe to predict that in times of distress, panic selling is highly likely to occur. Likewise, many other aspects of investment behavior in the market can be anticipated beforehand. Elliott argued that a lot of effort had gone into predicting the stock market, but most had failed because the human factor was not brought into consideration while making predictions about the future. He proposed that human behavior, which is not always consistent, should be at the center of stock market analysis. To Elliott, human beings were not programmed to act rationally on every single occasion, but their behavior followed certain patterns or rhythms that are inherent in nature.

Elliott considered every stock price movement to be a part of grander cyclic movements that span a larger time frame. Since, to him, all present market activities are part of a larger story, they have to be connected to past market activities, and future market activities also would be connected to the present. Coming back to our theme of technical analysis, history matters and history repeats itself. Elliott meticulously analyzed historical data about DJIA movements since the average's inception until the mid-1940s and concluded that market movements exhibit some regular patterns that were *wavelike*. He accepted that the possible permutations and combinations of such wavelike movements were numerous and that each wave was never exactly the same as any in the past. However, significant similarities did exist that could be used as a basis for predicting the nature of movements to come. The waves in Elliott theory, also known as *Elliott waves,* appear in regular sequences that follow certain mathematical properties associated with the famous Fibonacci numbers. This very interesting mathematical sequence will be discussed shortly in this chapter. Fibonacci numbers and ratios are closely tied to Elliott's projections of price movements and market timings. Although we have mentioned that Elliott waves appear in recognizable patterns, it is not a simple task to determine these patterns. These patterns can get very intricate, and it takes a keen sense of perception of market price movements to decipher the wave patterns.

In this chapter first we will discuss the patterns of the Elliott waves at length. We introduce the idea of Fibonacci numbers and Fibonacci ratios and discuss their relation to Elliott's projections concerning the relative lengths and strengths of waves. We also will touch on the temporal aspect of wave formation, i.e., how much time it takes for a particular trend to begin or end.

MAIN PRINCIPLES OF THE ELLIOTT WAVE THEORY

The Elliott wave theory contends that stock market price movements take place in repetitive cycles of similar structure. Every cycle is made up of two overarching movements. There is a wave in the direction of the primary trend, which is called an *impulsive wave*. This is followed by a wave in the opposite direction, which is called a *corrective wave*. The main wave in the direction of the primary trend has five smaller waves, and the main corrective wave has three smaller waves. Thus there are five waves in the direction of the primary trend, and these are followed by a three-wave correction in the opposite direction. This eight-wave or five-three cycle takes place over and over again. The relative lengths of the waves vary, but the basic eight-wave structure remains invariant. Each of the eight waves of a cycle in turn subdivides into smaller waves, which can be broken into even smaller waves. Very quickly we can break the system up into a pattern of waves embedded in larger waves, which in turn are embedded in even larger waves. And each cycle is also part of a larger cyclic structure.

Let us first discuss a cycle. Figure 7-1 will help us understand this better. We label the waves 1, 2, 3, 4, 5, *a, b,* and *c.* A five-wave impulse, or advance, takes the market price from 1 to 5. This is followed by a three-wave decline from *a* to *c.* Waves 1, 3, and 5 are called *impulsive waves* because they propel the price in the direction of the chief trend, which in this case is upward. Waves 2 and 4 move in the opposite direction of the advances made by waves 1 and 3. They are called *corrective waves.* Notice that waves 2 and 4 are corrective waves within the larger impulsive wave that goes from 1 to 5. Waves *a* to *c* that correct the overall advance made by impulse waves 1 through 5 are also corrective.

By definition, impulsive waves are stronger than the corrective waves. Wave 2 never outdoes the movement of wave 1 but retraces only a proportion of it. Likewise, wave 4 never outdoes wave 3. At the end of wave 4 the price is always at a higher point than where it was at the end of wave 2. Thus wave 4 moves upward from a point above the lowest tip of wave 2. In addition, Elliott predicted that wave 3 usually was larger than waves 1 and 5. This is something we will turn to later in this chapter.

While the waves from 1 to *c* have taken the market to a higher level, notice the intermediate "hiccups," or corrections. This may remind you of the Dow theory's interpretation of the market, where primary trends are corrected by secondary trends. Not only this. You may remember that according to Dow, the bull or the bear market has three phases. Elliott wave movements are strikingly similar. In the main movement from waves 1 to 5 in Figure 7-1, there are three phases when the price rises with two intermediate corrections. The three phases can be compared to the beginning, the main portion, and the ending of a bullish market. In addition, we mentioned that Elliott postulated that wave 3 tends to be longer than waves 1 and 5. This is in harmony with the Dow concept that the most sustained gain (or loss) in the market is made during the second phase of the bullish (or bearish) market.

Each of the eight waves shown in Figure 7-1 has smaller waves within it. Let's try to follow the smaller picture. Just as waves 1 through 5 and *a* through *c* made up a cycle, waves 1 and 2 by themselves make up a

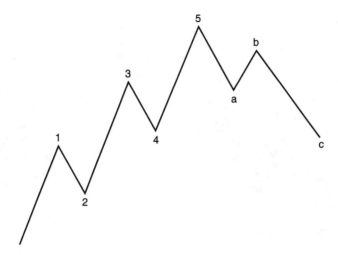

Figure 7-1 The basic wave pattern.

smaller cycle. In this cycle, since the gain made by wave 1 is greater than the decline due to wave 2, wave 1 would be the impulse wave (main trend) and wave 2 the correction. Waves in the direction of the main trend are always made up of five smaller waves, and corrective waves are made up of three waves. Just as in the big picture, i.e., the main trend divided into five waves, here wave 1 will have five waves within it, whereas the correction, i.e., wave 2, will be subdivided into three waves. Likewise, waves 3 through *c* will be subdivided into smaller waves. If we count them, the number of waves totals to 34.

Figure 7-2 shows the subdivision into 34 waves. Waves 1* and 2* are the initial large waves. Impulse wave 1* is subdivided into five waves (1 through 5). Correction wave 2* is subdivided into three waves (*a* through *c*). The waves 1, 3, and 5 are moving in the direction of the main trend and are impulse waves. Thus they are each divided into five smaller waves. Waves 2 and 4, on the other hand, are corrections, and each is divided into three smaller waves. These five waves then have 21 (i.e., 5 + 3 + 5 + 3 + 5) smaller waves. Now notice carefully the subdivision of waves *a, b,* and *c*. Waves *a* and *c* are going with the downward trend in the larger wave 2*, and they are impulsive within wave 2*. Thus they will each be divided into five smaller waves. However, within wave 2*, wave *b* is the wave going counter to the downward trend and will have

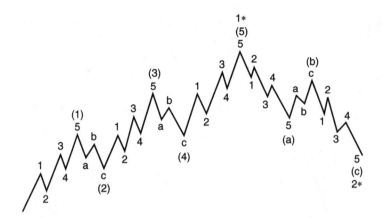

Figure 7-2 Waves and subwaves.

three subwaves. These three subwaves then have 13 (i.e., 5 + 3 + 5) smaller waves. On the whole, waves 1 through *c* have 34 (i.e., 21 + 13) smaller waves. By a similar process, these 34 waves can be divided into 144 smaller waves. This is so because the 21 waves from waves 1 through 5 subdivide into 89 waves, and the 13 waves from waves *a* through *c* subdivide into 55 waves. And all these waves can be divided further still.

The breaking up of the waves into smaller waves follows a pattern that matches the Fibonacci sequence. The Fibonacci sequence is a series of numbers: 1, 1, 2, 3, 5, 8, 13, 21, 34, 55, 89, 144, 233, and so on. Notice that the numbers of this sequence appear with regularity in the Elliott wave disaggregation. Elliott's theory would be very simple if what we described earlier explained all its nuances. However, there are significant variations in real-world stock market patterns. We describe these patterns later in this chapter. Interpreting waves properly is crucial to using the wave theory properly. For example, if we know we are in a bull market and there is a five-wave downturn, we must not consider it to be corrective waves 2 or 4. It might well be the end of the bull market, with the five-wave impulsive wave going in the opposite direction. Alternatively, it could just be the first three waves of a correction, sending us a signal that more downward price adjustments are in store. Interpreting the waves involves a lot of subjective judgments, and the deeper an individual's understanding is of the market and of the Elliot wave theory, the more likely he or she is to be accurate in making subjective assessments.

WAVE LEVELS

All waves have different relative sizes, and waves exist in different levels. Elliott argued that there were nine such levels of waves. The largest to the smallest can be listed as grand supercycle, supercycle, cycle, primary, secondary, minor, minute, minuette, and subminuette. The grand super-cycle was as long as a couple of hundred years, whereas the subminuette covered only a couple of hours of market activity. The middle three waves, the primary, secondary, and minor waves, are akin to Dow's mar-ket trends. Elliott considered that he had improved on Dow's ideas by disaggregating price movements more finely.

Elliott's idea of cyclic patterns in the market was not entirely unique. Several contemporary economists also held the view that the economy went through well-defined cycles over time. Toward the end of the nine-teenth century, economist Stanley Jevans argued that the economy went through 10-year cycles. In the 1920s, Russian economist Nikolai Kon-dratieff proposed a 54-year economic cycle that came to be known as the *Kondratieff cycle*. He analyzed whatever limited data he had and con-cluded that the economies of the modern capitalist countries tend to go through a cycle of expansion and contraction that lasts around 54 years. In the middle of the 1930s, Joseph Schumpeter combined the work of three economists, Juglar, Kitchen, and Kondratieff. Juglar had suggested an 18-year cycle, and Kitchen had suggested a 4-year cycle. Schumpeter argued that a Kondratieff cycle was made up of 3 Juglar cycles or 14 Kitchen cycles. It seems doubtful that Elliott was aware of these devel-opments in economics because he made no mention of them in his work. This makes his idea of cycles and waves in the stock market all the more remarkable (in fact, it is interesting to note that what Elliott classified as a supercycle corresponds closely with the Kondratieff cycle in terms of duration). Elliot conceptualized market activity as a phenomenon that was remarkably well organized and connected through time. His subdivisions of cycles were a lot more detailed than those of the economists. Whereas economists talked of cycles being as brief as 4 years, Elliott's shortest cycle could be as short as a few hours. Of course, the mechanisms the economists and Elliott used to come up with the characterization of cycles had hardly anything in common with one another. The economists who came up with the concept of economic cycles did so by imposing fixed time frames on market and economic behavior. Elliott did not believe in such fixed time frames within which market actions would be repeated.

To him, the aggregate stock market cycle was not bound by rigid repetitive time cycles.

FIBONACCI NUMBERS

The waves in the Elliott wave theory seem to appear in the numerical sequence discovered by a thirteenth-century Italian mathematician named Leonardo Fibonacci da Pisa. Elliott argued that the stock market had a natural tendency to act in ways that are consistent with many properties of the Fibonacci sequence.

Fibonacci numbers begin with 1 and continue to infinity. As mentioned, they appear in the sequence 1, 1, 2, 3, 5, 8, 13, 21, 34, 55, 89, 144, 233, ... Except for the initial number 1, each Fibonacci number is the addition of the preceding two numbers in the sequence. Thus the numbers derived as follows:

$$
\begin{aligned}
1 & \\
1 &= 0 + 1 \\
2 &= 1 + 1 \\
3 &= 1 + 2 \\
5 &= 2 + 3 \\
8 &= 3 + 5 \\
13 &= 5 + 8 \\
21 &= 8 + 13 \\
34 &= 13 + 21 \\
55 &= 21 + 34 \\
89 &= 34 + 55 \\
144 &= 55 + 89 \\
&\quad\cdot \\
&\quad\cdot \\
&\quad\cdot
\end{aligned}
$$

Let's recall our bullish cycle example to see the similarities between Elliot waves and Fibonacci numbers. Remember that every cycle has 2 main waves, one advance and one decline. The advance has 5 waves, and the decline has 3 waves. At this level, the cycle has 8 waves. Each of the 5 advancing waves has 21 smaller waves, and each of the 3 declining waves has 13 smaller waves. The cycle has 34 waves at that level. The 21 waves in their turn have 89 even smaller waves, and the 13 waves have 55 smaller waves. At this level of calculation, the cycle has 144 waves. The number of waves in different levels—2, 3, 5, 8, 13, 21, 34, 55, 89, 144—are all Fibonacci numbers.

This is just the relationship of Elliot wave patterns to Fibonacci numbers. Let us mention some ratios of Fibonacci numbers that are of significance to Elliott waves. Fibonacci ratios are tied to the relative lengths of these waves. We will explain the connection later in this chapter, but for now, we just mention them.

For the first four Fibonacci numbers, the ratios of each number divided by its next number are 1 (i.e., $\frac{1}{1}$), 0.50 (i.e., $\frac{1}{2}$), 0.67 (i.e., $\frac{2}{3}$), and 0.60 (i.e., $\frac{3}{5}$). After the first four numbers, we see some remarkably consistent properties among the Fibonacci numbers. For example, after the first four numbers, if we divide each number by its next higher number, the ratio is roughly 0.618. For example, $\frac{8}{13}$ is 0.615, $\frac{13}{21}$ is 0.619, and so on. Inversely, if we divide each number by its preceding number (e.g., $\frac{13}{8}$ or $\frac{21}{13}$), the ratio is around 1.618 ($\frac{1}{0.618}$). Another important property of Fibonacci numbers is that the ratios of alternate numbers are around 2.618 (i.e., $\frac{55}{21} = 2.619$) or its inverse, 0.382 (i.e., $\frac{21}{55} = 0.382$).

The Fibonacci sequence describes many natural phenomena such as the proportion of animal life, the formation of flowers, the structure of buildings and music, etc. Attempting to link it to the stock market takes quite a leap of faith. Especially for the believers in the efficient-market hypothesis (EMH), the idea that the stock market has identifiable patterns that also are linked to something as esoteric as the Fibonacci sequence would seem ridiculous. Elliott, for his part, believed in a fundamental natural order of things. Since many natural and human phenomena apparently can be explained by the Fibonacci form, he strongly felt that its patterns could be applicable to stock market movements. As long as prices were not fixed by the government but were determined by market forces, Elliott felt his theory to have merit.

FORECASTING WITH THE ELLIOTT WAVE THEORY: A SIMPLE EXAMPLE

Before we get into more of the details of Elliot waves, let's consider a simple example of how to predict future market movements using its tools. Suppose that the DJIA is at 8000. Now a wave 1 advance takes it to 8100. What do we anticipate the next move to be? We know that wave

2 does not correct all of wave 1's advance. Thus, in the next move, the stock price would not be lower than 8000. Suppose that the downturn of wave 2 were 30. Now the market would be at 8070. This is a good time to buy because we know that wave 3 will take the market to a greater height. Suppose that after wave 3 the market peaks at 8300, a gain of 230. We know that wave 4 will move downward, but the market will not fall by more than 230. To guess how much it will decline, a good reference point is to look at the decline of wave 2. Following a gain of 100 by wave 1, wave 2 caused the market to decline by 30. A rough rule of thumb would be that for the gain of 230 resulting from wave 3, wave 4 will cause a decline of around 60 points. It may be more or less, but we can estimate it to be around 60 by looking at past history. Regardless, we know the result will not be lower than 8070.

Suppose that the DJIA in fact declined by 70 after wave 4 took place and ended up at 8230 points. Now we anticipate the market to rise again with wave 5. However, investors will be jittery because the wave 5 gain usually is offset by subsequent corrective waves. An investor still may buy at 8230 and unload the stocks as soon as he or she sees the market turning, which would signal the end of wave 5. Suppose that in wave 5 the DJIA rose by 120 to 8350. We know the good times are about to end. After wave 5, there will be a decline followed by an increase. According to the Elliot principle, usually the corrective force of the wave following wave 5 is the strongest. Thus an investor could assume that the market will decline by over 70 points (which was the wave 4 fall). The investor thus would not buy until the market has fallen at least 70 points after reaching its peak of 8350. After this fall, the investor could buy because the market would again rise temporarily. A less active investor may just decide to hang up his or her gloves after the wave 5 surge by selling near the peak and sitting out the three-wave correction phase.

There is more to market forecasting using Elliot waves than what this example illustrates. Elliott wave theory actually claims to provide precise ratios of the different waves in a cycle, which we will discuss later in this chapter. Still, we hope from this simple example that you get the gist of the broad principle of using the Elliot wave theory. While you cannot use these principles to ascertain for sure where the market will be exactly after each wave, you can at least form a rough idea of the minimum or maximum extent of each move. This itself could be a powerful tool for investing.

IMPULSIVE WAVES

Earlier in this chapter we defined *impulsive waves* as the waves moving in the direction of the main trend. Corrective waves were in a sense the irritants or speed breakers to impulsive waves. Impulsive waves are relatively easy to figure out compared with corrective waves. There are two main types of impulsive waves: impulses and diagonal triangles.

Impulses

An *impulse* is the more common of the two impulsive waves. It is different from a diagonal triangle because in an impulse, wave 4 and wave 1 do not have overlapping price levels. Note the subtlety here. Previously, when we broadly characterized impulsive waves, we said that the bottom of wave 4 must be above the bottom of wave 2, meaning that the move by wave 3 must surpass the correction by wave 4. Here we are talking about a stronger condition. The move by wave 3 must outdo the move by wave 4 to such an extent that wave 1 and wave 4 should not overlap. An impulse is the strongest form of an impulsive wave. We essentially drew Figure 7-1 in such a manner that it illustrates an impulse. Notice that in it waves 1 and 4 do not overlap. In their book, A. J. Frost and Robert Prechter further add that waves 1, 3, and 5 of an impulse are *impulsive subwaves* (also called *actionary subwaves*), with wave 3 itself being an impulse. Thus in an impulse we would expect wave 3 to be the strongest force that propels the market.

Of the characteristics of impulses, *extension* and *truncation* are two important ones that we will discuss here. The properties of *alternation* and *channeling,* which are also of tremendous importance, are left for later sections.

Extension. Elliott believed that impulses usually contained extensions. An *extension* is a lengthened impulse with a disproportionate number of subwaves. What this means is that of the three actionary subwaves, one of them may have a length or duration that is much longer than the other four waves. It may even be as prominent as all the other four waves put together. The wave with an extension usually is subdivided into five waves itself. Then, on the whole, the larger impulse will have nine waves, four original waves plus five from the extension.

Of the three impulsive waves, normally only one can have extensions. Thus, if wave 3 had extensions, waves 1 and 5 would not. If wave 1 had extensions, waves 1 and 5 would not, and if neither wave 1 nor wave 3 had extensions, there is a good chance that wave 5 may have extensions. In the stock market, usually wave 3 is the one that most frequently has extensions. This is not surprising because in a bearish or bullish trend most activity takes place in the middle phase. Thus we can expect wave 3 to have extensions. Figure 7-3 shows a bull market with a wave 3 extension. It often is difficult to identify an extension. It could be the case that an entire impulse is composed of nine virtually indistinguishable waves.

Truncation. *Truncation* refers to a situation in which a market's projected upward or downward progress is unexpectedly halted. Thus, in a bullish market, if wave 5 fails to take price past the height attained by wave 3, we would call it a *truncated fifth.* Alternatively, in a bear market, if wave 5 does not sink to a level lower than wave 3, it would be a truncation. A truncation is likely to be a signal that a bull market may be weakening or that a bear market may be ending. Usually it is the case that after truncation takes place the bull market loses its vitality because it failed to break a particular resistance level. Alternatively, in a bearish market, the atmosphere may remain weak in general, but things may not be getting much worse as a downward slide is being halted by a certain support price.

Diagonal Triangles/Wedges

A *diagonal triangle* is an impulsive wave, but it is not as strong as an impulse. The corrective forces are more pronounced in it. As in any impulsive wave, here the corrections never fully recover the length of the preceding actionary wave. In this form also wave 3 is the longest, but it differs from an impulse because in it waves 1 and 4 overlap. That is, the lowest point of wave 4 would be lower than the highest point of wave 1. There are two forms of diagonal triangles: ending and leading.

Ending Diagonal. *Ending diagonals* tend to signal the end of a larger trend by moderating its advancement. They usually occur in wave 5 when wave 3 may have moved a bit too much and wave 4 perhaps did not correct much of that move. The market is now taking its time to moderate

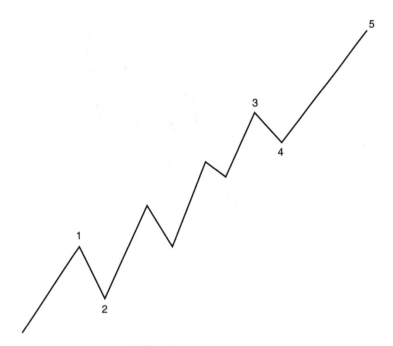

Figure 7-3 Wave 3 extension in a bull market.

the advance by wave 3 by creating obstacles to the progress of wave 5. Sometimes ending diagonals also occur in wave c.

Figure 7-4 illustrates an ending diagonal in a bull market. Wave 5 itself breaks into five waves, which, in turn, break into three smaller waves each. As a result, wave 5 has a 3-3-3-3-3 formation. Note that initially there is a lot of movement, both upward and downward, within wave 5, but it soon gets moderate. Thus, within wave 5, the rise and decline of waves 4 and 5 are less pronounced than the rise and decline of waves 1 and 2. If we draw two boundary lines, one connecting the peaks of waves 1, 3, and 5 and the other the troughs of waves 2 and 4, we would notice that the lines converge. This signals a weakening in wave 5's trend and the larger overall trend.

Leading Diagonal. In contrast to ending diagonals, *leading diagonals* occur in wave 1 or in wave *a*. These waves break into a 5-3-5-3-5 formation, which is different from the 3-3-3-3-3 formation of ending diagonals. Although here also the two boundary lines converge as in the case

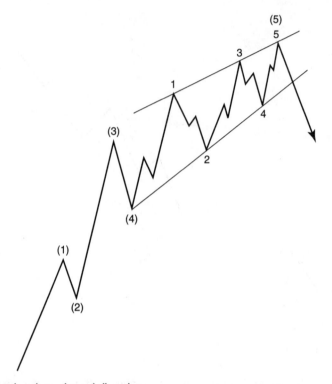

Figure 7-4 Ending diagonal in a bull market.

of ending diagonals, the conclusion we draw about the larger trend is just the opposite. Leading diagonals signal the continuation and not the weakening of the larger trend.

Now that we have discussed impulsive waves, we turn our attention to corrective waves.

CORRECTIVE WAVES

Corrective waves tend to be more complex and generally harder to identify than impulsive waves. This is so because their flows are not as smooth as those of the impulsive waves that just move in the direction of the larger trend. Often due to their complexity, corrective waves cannot be identified before an entire cycle is over. Thus it is important to try to approach a corrective or lackadaisical phase of the market with greater caution than a phase where the market is clearly being dominated by

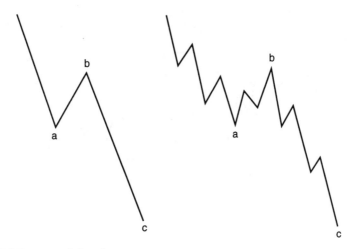

Figure 7-5 Zigzag in a bull market.

impulsive forces. Corrective waves are distinguishable from impulsive waves because they always have three subwaves, with the triangle formation being the lone exception to this rule.

There are four main groupings of corrective waves: zigzags, flats, triangles, and double-threes and triple-threes. We discuss each in turn.

Zigzags

Zigzags are the most straightforward of the corrective wave patterns. There are three types of zigzag moves: single, double, and triple. The *single zigzag* is the corrective wave we have illustrated so far. It is the simple three-wave declining pattern in a bull market and the three-wave increasing pattern in a bear market. The three waves break down into a 5-3-5 subwave formation. Figure 7-5 shows the form of a zigzag for a bull market. The bear market zigzag would be just the opposite and is often referred to as an *inverted zigzag.*

Often zigzags occur more than once. If a zigzag occurs twice, it is a *double zigzag,* and if it occurs three times, it is a *triple zigzag.* In such cases, each zigzag with a 5-3-5 formation is separated by one or two three-wave cycles. Looking at Figure 7-6 clarifies this. It is an example of a double zigzag. In it two zigzag formations *a-b-c* are separated by a three-wave formation going from wave *c* to wave 1. In a sense, the double zigzag is like the extensions we discussed in terms of impulse waves. We can think of *a-b-c* as being one wave, waves *c* through 1 as being another

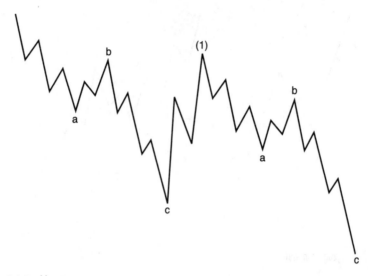

Figure 7-6 Double zigzag.

wave, and *a-b-c* as being the final wave. Thinking this way, we still get a three-wave correction, but with each wave having extensions.

Flats

A *flat* is relatively straightforward. It is a three-wave pattern with a 3-3-5 formation. As the correction begins, the first wave *a* does not have the vigor to break up into five waves. It instead breaks up into three waves. The second wave *b* breaks up into three small waves, and at the end, wave *c* divides into five waves. Let's take the bull market example (Figure 7-7). In it, wave *a* would drop moderately only, forming three subwaves. This drop is corrected almost fully by wave *b*, which also forms three subwaves. Finally, wave *c* follows a five-wave downward progression. However, wave *c* is also not very strong, and it ends just slightly below the end of wave *a*. In a bear market, the waves move in the opposite direction.

Flats are different from zigzags because they have a 5-3-5 formation. In addition, zigzags correct more sharply for impulsive waves, whereas flats are relatively toothless corrections. They follow periods of dynamic larger trends and provide only feeble resistance. The stronger the main trend is, the weaker the flats would be. Just as there are double zigzags,

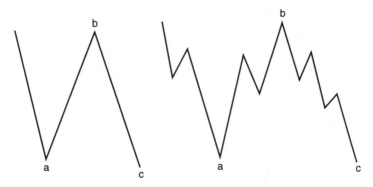

Figure 7-7 Flats in a bull market.

there are also *double flats*. These are also known as *double threes,* and
we will discuss them shortly.

Flats can have as many as three variations: regular flat, expanded flat,
and running flat. A *regular flat* is pretty much the correction we have
described so far. Wave *b* ends up at roughly the same level where wave
a began, and then wave *c* ends slightly past wave *a*. In the real market,
however, it is very common to observe expanded flats. This formation
appears a bit odd. Wave *b* actually covers more ground than wave *a;* i.e.,
it more than fully corrects for wave *a*. So far we have only discussed
forms with corrections less than impulses. Finally, wave *c* emerges as the
most powerful of all waves, and it proceeds more than wave *b* did (in the
opposite direction to wave *b*). As a result, it goes beyond the point where
wave *a* ended. Figure 7-8 shows an expanded flat for a bull market.

The *running flat* is another interesting formation. Wave *b* is very
dominant here, and as in an expanded flat, it dominates wave *a*. As a
result, it changes the price far away from the bottom of wave *a*. Wave *c*
moves in the opposite direction to wave *b,* but it cannot outdo the length
of wave *b*. As a result, the correction against the larger trend is very
limited. This would tend to be the case when the larger trend is very
strong.

Triangles
Triangles usually occur in wave 4 just before the final impulsive wave.
They also can occur in wave *b,* again just before the impulsive wave *c*.
Triangles lead to a sideways movement, implying a balance between com-

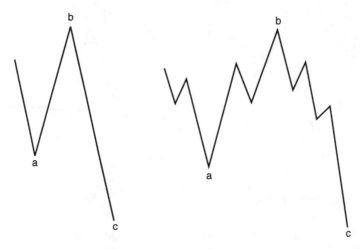

Figure 7-8 Expanded flat in a bull market.

peting trends. The wave preceding the triangle was an impulsive wave, and since a triangle is largely a sideways movement, it does not correct much of that impulsive move. It thus tends to be a period of consolidation. Since its movement is sideways, the waves composing it overlap. Triangles are made up of five waves, and each wave has three subwaves, giving the triangle a 3-3-3-3-3 form. The discussion of triangles here is similar to their discussion in Chapter 4. The ideas are the same, except that the discussion in Chapter 4 was not in terms of waves and cycles.

There are four classifications of triangles: ascending, descending, symmetrical, and contracting and expanding. The first three are termed *regular triangles*. In regular triangles, instead of waves fluctuating up and down in widening cycles, the waves fluctuate up and down in narrower cycles. This is evident from Figure 7-9, which shows triangle formations for a bull market. It is apparent that most of the subwaves in a triangle look like zigzags.

When a triangle occurs in wave 4, one can predict the likely characteristics of wave 5. It generally would move rapidly and cover roughly the distance of the widest part of the triangle. A triangle is constructed by connecting the end points of waves *a* and *c* and waves *b* and *d*. Wave *e* is usually not on the triangle boundary, especially for symmetrical and expanding triangles. Triangles also can predict the turning point of the market. The time it takes for the boundaries of a nonexpanding triangle to converge is roughly the time around when the market will start turning.

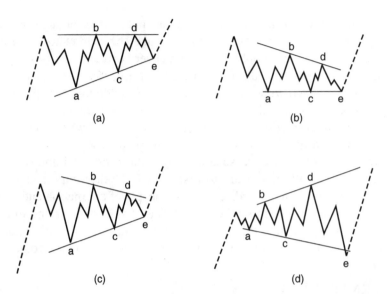

Figure 7-9 Triangle formations in a bull market: (*a*) ascending; (*b*) descending; (*c*) symmetrical; and (*d*) expanding.

From our discussion of diagonal triangles, recall that such a pattern was impulsive but not really very strong. The corrective forces were rather strong in it. Conversely, in the case of triangles, just the inverse is true. The impulsive forces are reasonably strong, blunting the actions of this corrective wave.

Double Threes and Triple Threes

These are combined structures of corrective waves. *Double-* or *triple threes* are formed by different combinations of simpler corrective wave-forms such as zigzags, flats, and triangles. Thus a zigzag may combine with a flat to form a double three. Double and triple threes are mostly sideways or horizontal movements, essentially leaving the price at the same level as before the correction took place. In this sense, they are like flats, except that they are longer in duration and magnitude. While it is possible theoretically for double or triple threes to run strongly counter to the larger trend, this is not usually the case in reality. This is so because they never seem to be composed of more than one zigzag formation.

We know that double- or triple-zigzag formations can have strong corrective features. They are strongly nonhorizontal. One of the reasons they occur is because the initial zigzag did not correct enough and the subsequent zigzags must correct more to take the market to its proper position. However, in a double three, whatever correction had to happen would have happened in the first corrective form, say, the zigzag. This correction is coupled with other corrections to form double or triple threes only to prolong the initial correction, not to add to its magnitude. In this case, the initial correction is a pretty good indicator of where the market wants to be, and this is why it is staying there for a while.

We have discussed at reasonable length the different impulsive and corrective forms. We now want to discuss a few other important issues in wave formation. First, we discuss the concepts of alternation and channeling. We also will touch on the importance of volume in trying to read patterns. It is only natural that volume would be linked to wave formation because it is linked to so much of what technical analysis is about.

ALTERNATION

This is a very broad concept. It essentially says that corrective patterns tend to alternate. Thus, if a particular pattern such as a flat occurred in the last corrective wave, it is likely that it will not occur in the next corrective wave. The principle of alternation helps us predict what is not likely to happen in the next wave. By providing us with this information, it helps us narrow down our choices as to what actually could happen next. There really is no sound logic to the occurrence of alternation, but empirical evidence from the stock market seems to suggest that exceptions to it are truly rare.

Let's consider an example of alternation within impulses. If wave 2 was a sharp correction, we would expect that wave 4 will be a weak correction, making the market move sideways. If wave 2, on the other hand, was a weak correction, wave 4 is likely to be a sharp correction. Figure 7-10 shows this. Another example of alternation would be that a zigzag correction is likely to be followed by a more horizontal correction such as a flat, a triangle, or a double- or triple-three.

CHANNELING

Channeling is the two lines that technicians draw on the sides (upside and downside) of the market price movement range. These lines together form a channel for the stock price to travel through. In an ascending

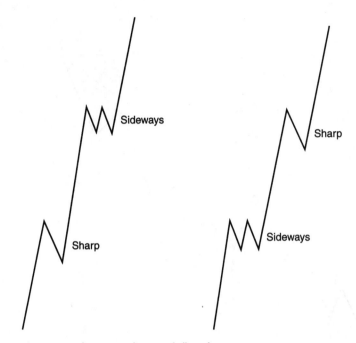

Figure 7-10 Alternation within an impulse (in a bull market).

market, it is like an upward-sloping rectangle, and in a descending market, it is like a downward-sloping rectangle.

Elliott used similar price channels to aid him in the numbering of waves. He observed that price channels tend to contain impulsive wave formations. One could then draw channels in advance to predict the range and direction of future price movements. To start off, we need three points to construct a channel. As shown in Figure 7-11, the channel is formed by a line connecting the tip of impulsive waves 1 and 3 and a line parallel to this that begins at the bottom of wave 2. Now we have an approximation of what wave 4 might look like. We would expect wave 4 to lie on or close to this channel. If wave 4 does not stay on the channel boundaries, we need to draw a new channel for the updated estimated direction of upcoming wave 5. The new channel would be a line connecting the bottoms of waves 2 and 4 and a parallel line from the tip of wave 3. This is shown in Figure 7-12. The point of drawing this channel is to help us project wave 5. We would expect wave 5 to end near the upper limits of the channel. If wave 3 exhibits an unusually sharp jump, it is probably a better idea to draw the upper line of the channel along the tip of wave 1.

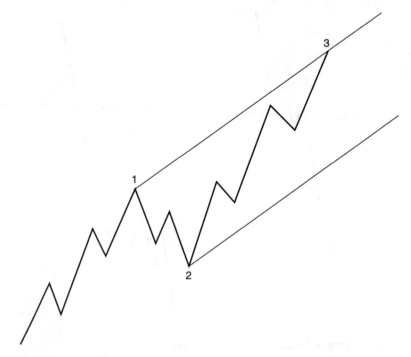

Figure 7-11 Initial channel.

It is probably more stable than wave 3, and it is likely that the market price will gravitate more toward the trend projected by it.

Elliott suggested using semilog functions to normalize prices and then drawing channels to get a more accurate depiction of future price movements. When semilog functions are applied to prices, they get smaller in value. As a result, fluctuations in the semilogs of prices are smaller than fluctuations in just the prices. Such a moderately fluctuating series can be represented more easily by drawing a channel. We do not have to keep updating the channels frequently because the price is bouncing so much.

VOLUME

Volume can be used to confirm wave counts and project future waves. We know from our general discussion in this book that volume levels go hand in hand with market vitality. In a bullish market, the volume rises

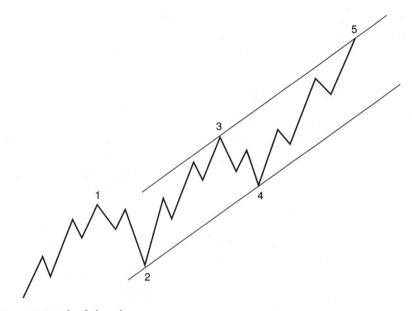

Figure 7-12 Updated channel.

and falls with price increases and declines. We would expect the volume level in wave 2 to be less than that in wave 1. In wave 3, volume level again picks up and would be greater than the volume level in wave 1. This is the likely case because wave 3 is similar to the second phase of the bull market that Dow talked about when the most sustained price increases take place accompanied by heavy trading by bullish investors. In wave 4, the volume would decline again, and finally, wave 5 would see a surge in volume. Toward the beginning of wave 5, the volume level is probably the highest, with the maximum number of investors trading in the market. Trading activity in wave 5 gradually would slow down as the market begins to show signs of turning. In wave 5, divergences between price changes and volume would start to develop, which is a sign of changing market conditions. A couple of things may happen. Price increases may not be accompanied by significant increases in volume as investors prepare for the downturn to kick in. Or price may remain relatively stable, say, rising slowly, but accompanied by heavy volume. Despite heavy interest in the market, investors do not really know where the price is heading, and as a result, the price fails to climb. These are the likely characteristics of volume levels in the different waves in a bull market. In a bearish market, contrary to a bullish market, price falls are accompanied by heavy volume and rises by moderate volume.

READING WAVES RIGHT

This is the biggest challenge to the technician. How does an investor decide what waveform the market is in? Often novice followers of Elliott waves mislabel waves and as a result are incorrect in their predictions of the market. To predict the future using Elliot waves, one must know present and past trends well. If individuals are mislabeling waves, then they are not reading the market's past and present right. How can they then reasonably predict anything about the future? If it is the case that an individual is reading the waves wrong, then he or she will expect price to act in one way, and it may end up acting in a different way, having unintended consequences for the investor. If he or she keeps reading waves wrong but acting on the basis of his or her readings anyway, pretty soon he or she will become a pauper.

In this section we take a look at a couple of examples of mislabeling. This should give you a sense of the kinds of mistakes you may make while trying to interpret waves. Also, you should get a sense of the many different combinations of labeling that are possible and how labeling correctly is not really an easy task. It is like solving a complex puzzle. Besides having a clear idea of the possible variations in Elliot waveforms, to get a sense of what sorts of wave counts make sense in the real world, an investor must have an intuitive sense of what has been going on in the real stock market besides knowing about the movements in the DJIA. Otherwise, an investor can end up reading waves too technically just to make them fit the Elliott form, and if the investor finds a way to make them fit, he or she will consider that to be a correct wave count. Yet many different wave formations may make sense for the particular price pattern the individual is looking at. Knowledge of the market at present and in the past is thus useful while counting or labeling waves.

Let's now look at some relatively simple examples of counting waves wrong. Suppose that a technician were to identify the formation in Figure 7-13 as an impulse. The wave does move in an upward direction, and it has five subwaves. What is wrong with this identification? In an impulse, waves 1 and 4 cannot overlap, as they do in the figure. Furthermore, in the figure, wave 3 is longer than wave 1, which is also an anomaly for

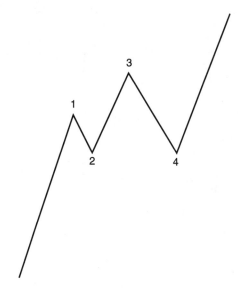

Figure 7-13 Incorrect labeling.

an impulse. Thus, clearly, the technician is identifying the waves incorrectly.

Let's look at Figure 7-14 for another example of incorrect labeling. We have labeled Figure 7-14*a* as a downward-moving impulsive wave that has five subwaves. However, this cannot be the case because wave 3 is shorter than waves 1 and 5. Now let's try to modify the labeling to make it consistent with Elliott principles. It may be that we are in a bearish market, and it is simply part of a three-wave correction to a five-wave advance. The first two corrections are waves 1 and 2, and we are in the third subwave of wave 3 with another two subwaves to come. Figure 7-14*b* shows the correct labeling.

Figure 7-15*a* gives another example of mislabeling. It shows a form called the *irregular top*. After wave 5, in the correction phase, the price actually gained in value. This is not typically the case in the market. We can have labeling that makes more sense to us. A possible labeling that makes sense is shown in Figure 7-15*b*, where the waves are part of a five-wave impulse in a bullish market.

This ends our discussion of the different forms of Elliot waves. Now we discuss briefly how to graph waves. Elliott himself used hourly data from the DJIA for his charts. Followers of his theory also tend to do the

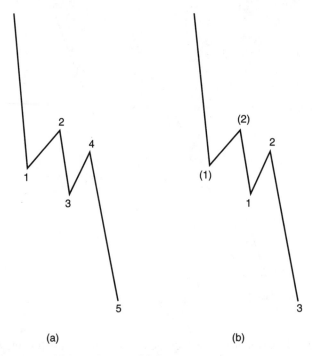

(a)   (b)

Figure 7-14 (*a*) Incorrect labeling. (*b*) Correct labeling.

same. Such data are easy to come by on the Internet or in newspapers and magazines such as the *Wall Street Journal* or *Barron's*. Hourly fluctuations give the technicians a good sense of wave counts, and these counts are actually not that time-consuming to chart. The actual DJIA levels at particular times must be used for charting instead of using, say, opening or theoretical intraday DJIA levels that do not tell us where the DJIA is at any particular time. It is easier to read the market waves when the impulsive waves are in progression and taking the market to new territories. Corrective waves are harder to decipher. Veterans such as A. J. Frost and Robert Prechter caution analysts about wave counting during major corrective periods. These are times during which waves do complicated things, and relatively uninitiated analysts could be thoroughly confused by what's going on. They may as well sit out such periods and only enter the market during impulsive phases.

Elliott wave theorists also argue that it is best to use a semilog price scale to chart the DJIA. Semilog scales give an accurate sense of the

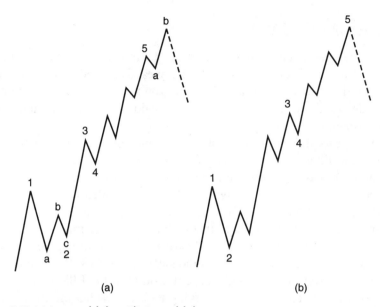

(a)   (b)

Figure 7-15 (*a*) Incorrect labeling. (*b*) Correct labeling.

percentage changes in the market average. Such percentage changes are what is really important to note in the market instead of calculating the absolute day-to-day change. Absolute changes in the DJIA do not really tell us much about changing market conditions over a long time horizon. In the 1960s, a 200-point decline in the DJIA would have been like the market getting pneumonia, but today, such a drop may not even qualify as a minor cold, whereas a 10 percent change in the DJIA in 1960 can be compared with a 10 percent change in today's market. Especially when we are comparing across long time horizons, it is essential to use the semilog scale.

In the next sections we move on to the relationship between Fibonacci ratios and the relative lengths of waves and issues concerning timing in the market. While the discussion of wave patterns is meant to give the analyst using Elliott principles a sense of where the market is heading, ratio analysis intends to be more precise in its projections of the future of the market. It tries to predict *how much* the market will move in any particular direction. The question of timing intends to improve the precision of forecasting using Elliot waves further by giving the analyst a sense of *when* a move is expected to happen.

RATIOS AMONG WAVES

We earlier mentioned a few properties of Fibonacci numbers and some ratios that are of relevance to Elliott waves. The ratios mentioned were 0.50, 0.618, 1.618, 2.618, and 0.382. If you wish to recall how the ratios were derived, you may go back to the section on Fibonacci numbers in this chapter.

It appears that a lot of Elliott wave principles are rather "magically" tied to the Fibonacci ratios. The famous Dow theorist Robert Rhea unwittingly provided a ratio that came close to the Fibonacci ratio 0.618. In his book, *The Story of Averages* (1936), he compiled data for the stock market from 1896 to 1932. Of the 13,115 active trading days in the market during this period, Rhea found that on 8143 days the market was bullish and on 4972 days the market was bearish. The ratio of bearish to bullish days was 0.61, very close to the Fibonacci ratio 0.618. While this figure could very likely be a coincidence, enthusiasts of the Elliott wave theory like to cite it as old evidence justifying their belief that the stock market does in fact demonstrate properties consistent with the Fibonacci ratios or, in other words, properties associated with the natural order of things.

When Elliott wave theorists refer to using Fibonacci ratios to calculate or predict the relative lengths of waves, they are usually thinking in terms of retracements and multiples. These concepts are described at length in A. J. Frost and Robert Prechter's book on Elliot waves.

Let's discuss retracements first. The Elliott theory states that a correction usually retraces a Fibonacci proportion (ratio) of its previous wave. Thus corrections are usually associated with Fibonacci ratios 0.382, 0.50, 0.618, and 1. A sharp correction may retrace as much as 0.50 or 0.618 of its previous wave. This is especially the case when the sharp correction occurs in wave 2. On the other hand, a weak or a sideways correction would retrace only about 0.382 of its previous wave. In particular, this is the likely case when a weak correction occurs in wave 4. Being able to predict the extent of retracements is what technical analysts would like. Suppose, for example, that wave 2 was a weak correction. Then technicians may expect that wave 4 will be a sharp correction. If wave 3 made the stock market gain 30 points, they would guess that wave 4 will correct this gain by around 18 points (30 multiplied by 0.618). If they are right in their estimates, they stand to gain a lot. Their decision would be to buy when the market falls around 18 points from its wave 4 peak.

Let's now turn to multiples. We earlier mentioned that only one of the three impulsive waves 1, 3, and 5 could have extensions. If wave 3 has an extension, which is usually the most likely, then the lengths of waves 1 and 5 are either the same, or one of them could be 0.618 of the other. Usually, it tends to be the case that all impulsive waves are proportional to each other by Fibonacci numbers 1, 1.618 (or its inverse 0.618), and 2.618 (or its inverse 0.382).

In the case of corrective waves, the ratios are different from the case of impulsive waves. In a zigzag correction, usually waves a and c are of the same length, although one of them may be 1.618 times the other. In a double zigzag, the relationship between the two zigzags is the same as the relationship between waves a and c in a single zigzag. In the case of a regular flat, waves a, b, and c are roughly the same length, with c perhaps being a bit longer. In an expanded flat, wave c is usually 1.618 times wave a. In fact, sometimes wave c can be as long as 2.618 times wave a. This is so because in an expanded flat, wave b terminates beyond the starting point of wave a, and wave c terminates beyond the end point of wave a. For this, wave c has to be longer than wave a. Recall Figure 7-8 to visualize this better.

In a triangle formation, Elliot theorists contend that Fibonacci relationships exist between alternative waves. This means that alternative waves are usually related to each other by a multiple of 0.618. More specifically, wave $e = 0.618c$, wave $c = 0.618a$, and wave $d = 0.618b$. These are the supposed relationships for ascending, descending, and symmetrical triangles. We know that the fluctuations of waves gradually get smaller in magnitude the longer the triangle pattern continues, and hence it is not a surprise that wave a is longer than wave c, which is longer than wave e. Nevertheless, it is interesting to note the supposed Fibonacci relationship among them.

In addition to these ratios, there are some other commonly used Fibonacci ratios that are by and large variations of what has just been discussed. In his book, *Technical Analysis of the Financial Markets*, John Murphy mentions a few of them:

By multiplying the length of wave 1 by 1.618 and adding that to the ending value of wave 2, we can estimate a minimum target for the top of wave 3.

By multiplying the length of wave 1 by 3.236 (1.618 × 2) and adding that value to the top or bottom of wave 1, we can get the maximum and minimum bounds for the top of wave 5.

When waves 1 and 3 are equal, wave 5 is expected to extend. By multiplying the distance from the beginning of wave 1 to the end of wave 3 by 1.618 and adding this to the bottom of wave 4, we can estimate the length of wave 5.

The length of wave *c* could be estimated by multiplying 0.618 to the length of wave *a* and subtracting this number from the bottom of wave *a*.

All these are possible ways of calculating the movements of waves. As you can tell by now, the guidelines or rules of thumb for such calculations are numerous and depend on the context of the market.

We remember that the Elliot wave theory is about waves embedded within waves. Thus at any given time in any given wave formation there could exist Fibonacci relationships at many different levels. When estimating the future trend of the market, the more levels of waves and their supposed Fibonacci relationships an analyst can take into account, the more accurate his or her forecast will be.

TIMING AND FIBONACCI NUMBERS

According to Elliott enthusiasts, the Fibonacci series can give analysts a sense of when to anticipate market turning points. The work done on this is not as extensive as the work on wave patterns and wave ratios. Elliott projections concerning market timing are considered relatively less reliable than the forecasts of wave patterns and ratios even by adherents of Elliott waves.

It is important to be consistent while making predictions concerning market timing. If an analyst wants to forecast the turning point of an intermediate wave, he or she must start at the end of the preceding intermediate wave and try to see what is likely to happen. It would be incorrect to start just at any random date and try to make an accurate projection of that intermediate wave. When Elliott followers try to predict the next major market move, they start from the end of the preceding move and predict the new move to happen in a manner related to the Fibonacci sequence. Thus from an important turning point they would expect the next top or bottom to happen in, say, 8, 13, 21, 34, or 55 days. The next market move could even be calculated in terms of hours or weeks. Suppose that the market is experiencing a short-term rally. An Elliott enthusiast may look at the market activity and predict that the rally will last for 3 or 5 hours. If the rally lasts for over 5 hours, the analyst probably would expect a correction to begin in the eighth hour. This is just one of the ways an analyst might form his or her expectations of the market movements if he or she is tied to Elliott principles.

CONCLUDING THOUGHTS ON WAVE THEORY

As mentioned at the outset of this chapter, the Elliott wave theory is similar to the Dow theory. Like Dow, Elliott also believed that stocks tend to move in groups and thus that a broad market indicator such as the DJIA signals what is likely to happen to the market as a whole. Since stocks move in groups, from the aggregate market behavior we could extrapolate information as to what is likely to happen to individual stock prices. For example, it is unlikely that if the broad market is bearish, the stock price of Coca-Cola will reach spectacular heights.

Charles Dow used metaphors of tides and waves to make his points about market movements. Elliott, on the other hand, used the concept of waves. Dow's three phases of a bull or bear market are quite similar to Elliott's conceptualization of three impulsive waves. The Dow theory employs the concept of confirmation (the two market averages, the DJIA and the Dow Jones Transportation Average, or DJTA, must align or conform with one another), which the Elliott wave theory lacks. However, Elliott felt that his theory was richer than Dow's and that it validated a lot of Dow's concepts. For example, one could look at Elliott wave formations in both the DJIA and the DJTA and predict when nonconfirmation was likely to take place. Conversely, by looking at the DJIA and DJTA concurrently, one can make some predictions about Elliott waves. For example, if the averages do not confirm each other, which as we know is a sign that the market may be turning, the analyst using Elliott waves could assume that an impulsive wave was about to weaken.

If we remember the discussion of the EMH from Chapter 3, we can naturally conclude that believers in the EMH would not think much of the Elliott wave theory. For followers of the EMH, future price movements are truly random events and beyond the scope of forecasting. Elliott wave theory runs completely counter to the EMH in that it contends that not only can price trends be predicted with a certain degree of certainty but so can their magnitudes and durations. It is difficult to say who is right because both sides tend to furnish information supporting their views. Believers in the EMH think that individuals using Elliott wave principles in the market will lose money. In rare cases, if they do succeed, it is likely due to "dumb luck." Followers of the EMH find it hard to swallow that Fibonacci ratios such as 1.618 can explain the relative lengths of waves or that Fibonacci days can predict when the market will turn. Elliott wave theorists argue that the stock market is a natural phenomenon and that there is nothing surprising in it following patterns that are common in nature. To them, the market is not a random phenomenon.

Given the inherent uncertainties surrounding any theory, it is probably wise for investors not to rely solely on any one theory. The same goes for the Elliott wave theory. It should be viewed as one of the many tools that analysts may use for success in the market. An analyst equipped with other technical and fundamental tools will be able to use the Elliott wave theory with greater expertise and wisdom and make fewer errors while labeling waves and trying to forecast the future.

C H A P T E R 8

QUESTIONS AND ANSWERS

As we have seen in previous chapters, technical analysis contains a strong interpretive component. The unfortunate situation in which two technicians looking at the same data but coming to completely different conclusions is all too common. Some technicians even suggest that the same person looking at the same chart but with the data inverted may come to a different conclusion than if the chart were held right side up. This sort of subjectivity is problematic for the process of learning technical analysis. It would not be beneficial for a beginner to learn technical analysis and at the same time learn the biases of the sources of their learning. The problem of bias in the presentation of a topic can be alleviated somewhat by presenting many different points of view.

Seeing many different points of view is like diversification. When one wants to reduce the risk of an investment, one diversifies one's portfolio so as to reduce the variance of the return. That is, by spreading one's money over many assets, one reduces the chances of losing money because while a particular asset may lose, it is improbable that they all will lose money. This is the age-old idea of not putting all of one's eggs in a single basket. The concept of diversifying one's investment to reduce the uncertainty of the return is not confined to the stock market, however.

One can view reading a book as an investment, where one invests time in learning about a topic. Accordingly, in order to better diversify the ideas presented in this book about the markets, this chapter includes a series of opinions on trading and investing by some friends and colleagues of the authors involved in direct access trading. By including their opinions to some frequently asked questions, this chapter serves to diversify the informational content and opinions on investing so as to not put all the reader's eggs in one basket either.

Q: Is it even realistic to expect to make money in the markets, where there are so many sophisticated traders and institutions trading day in and day out?

A: I think so, especially with the advent of computer-based trading, where the consumer has the opportunity to log on to the net and trade stocks at a low cost. I think it is important to stress that people really have an opportunity here. In the old days, one would pour over the books and figure out carefully what to do because one mistake, and you were out $60 or $130 on round-trip commissions to get out of the market. And that's not counting slippage, because by the time you made the call and the person on the other end felt like executing your deal, the stock was moving against you a few more points. It was really a nightmare, because, of course, you were in a hurry, when the stock was killing you, so the slowest service also came at the worst time. I think today people have the ability to manage their portfolios more intensely and to learn to make sound investments without having to worry about the slice you will lose to commissions and slippage. There is an important point that I would not want to go unsaid. I'm not saying that hard work before trading has become irrelevant, because that would be foolish. Thinking that commissions are low, so rash trading decisions can be fixed without major costs, would be an unwise strategy in my opinion. It is still an expensive proposition to be trading back and forth carelessly. What I mean is that if a mistake is made, speed and execution are available to remedy it, and at lower costs. These lower costs are also present when mistakes are not made and trades are going as planned, and this is as much an advantage for the trader.

Beyond this issue, however, there really is no reason to think that one should sit by and watch the market move without a prayer because one is not managing some multibillion dollar portfolio with a staff of 100. First of all, having a staff like that is no guarantee. Look at LTCM; they had a couple dozen Ph.D.s and have become the scapegoat of Wall Street. Everyone who wants to make the argument that less is more in terms of education drums up LTCM. And they did fail. I guess the lesson is that there are no guarantees. Small investors also have no guarantees, but they have a better opportunity to put their money somewhere where it is getting a decent rate of return. I think someone who looks at the markets with this sort of conservative approach will do well enough to learn how to make money and not worry about the larger business concerns that trade on Wall Street.

Q: With a small amount of investment capital, such as that of a small investor, what are some of the methods that one would choose?

A: I think that if someone has a small amount of money to begin with, they should concentrate on achieving reasonable goals and not trying to be George Soros or Hillary Rodham Clinton, turning $1000 into $100,000 in a year. Many friends I talk to go into the market and trade like it is their job, when they should be thinking about what they want. This goes back to what I was just saying, that just because one has more ability to trade, this does not give you a license to overtrade your profits away.

I think beginners and people who do not trade as a full-time job should try to learn as much as possible. With regard to the technical stuff, it is all really applicable regardless of the size of the investment. People look for turning points, and that really is independent of trade size, so it would apply to the small investor as much as to anyone. I think the danger here is that the small investor may forget to see the forest for the trees. The idea of having technical analysis is to have a guide for where to go. This does not solve the problem; I do not know anyone with crystal balls. It takes a lot of patience and management to succeed. If you think you have a quick answer to making money on the markets, I would be very interested to hear it—unless it's buy low and sell high.

Q: Is it safer for an individual to turn to a stock market professional rather than go it alone in the markets?

A: I do not think this is necessarily the case. I certainly would not want to answer yes. Who would be the professional that they turn to? There are lots of people out there who know what they are doing, at least in my humble opinion, but I am not sure that average family people in middle America have access to them. They are pricey professionals I am talking about. I am sure there are a lot of them out there, but frankly, not too many of them are managing savings accounts for two-income families. Usually they are managing the assets of some pension fund as part of a team of analysts or what have you. As a result, the individual faces a situation in which he or she has to face a responsibility.

The issue is whether the individual can sit down and look over the necessary information about the what, where, and how of investing. If not, then perhaps a professional is the way to go. There are also lots of companies that will meet you half way, with electronic brokers and also a little advice to give you a boost. I do not think they add that much, but for many people, it is enough to get them going. I would say that for many people getting started is the key. A man I know recently began investing on his own and was asking me questions on and off when we ran into each other. Nowadays, he comes up to me and tells me about his money and his latest acquisitions, as well as his outlook. It is fascinating to see someone with no background and no experience in finance become enveloped in the field and just go nuts with the stuff. Of course, it also makes a lot of sense. He is putting his money in there, so he is also putting in effort and time into making sure that the risks are well understood. If you are able to do that, a professional will be a waste of money. If you are not, a professional may end up saving you money.

Q: How does one approach the issue of forecasting stocks and estimating future stock prices?

A: Forecasting is serious business. Usually technical analysis serves to find a turning point, and if successful, one may then give oneself the luxury of forecasting. I think oftentimes people do not know how much guesswork goes into these things. There are plenty of pros out there with really complicated models—mathematical models that will knock your socks off. It is unbelievable what some of these people do. Some are doing fractal geometry, noninteger dimensional math, and chaos and turbulence theory; it is a total nightmare. On the other end of the spectrum there is the orangutan from California that apparently does as well as the investment advisers by just throwing darts at the *Wall Street Journal.* It is really amusing.

Usually if a price seems to be tracing out a pattern, implicit in that pattern is the next objective of the price, which is the standard forecast measurement of where the price should at least go. These are useful guides, but one should really keep an eye on the conditions day to day, because the price is tracing its pattern out with different market conditions each time, and there are adjustments that one could make. For example, if the Fed meets and leaves interest rates alone, a stock could be tracing out the clearest pattern in the world, and it may be obvious that it is bound to fall, but it temporarily should be boosted by the general market surge. There could be temporary interruptions occurring in the markets that cause this sort of thing, and they may skew a price movement one way or another. We should be able to correct for these sorts of minor disturbances in the price movement. The key here is to know what is a minor disturbance and what is a fundamental change.

Q: If you see a price pattern and you believe that it is completed, when do you jump in and buy on the buy signal and when do you sit and wait to see if the reversal is genuine? Do you base your decision on a price movement of a certain size or on a certain amount of time on the opposite side of the trend line?

A: In the case where I am following a price that is tracing out a nice trend line, and it looks like it is beginning to form a reversal pattern, the first step is to start looking for other evidence that the price is turning against the current trend. In a sense, what you want to look for is a sign that the market is changing its mind about how things are going with regard to this particular stock. If there is some fundamental news or earnings report coming out and this is affecting the stock, then this would be an obvious source of information to confirm a reversal. I am not opposed, by the way, to looking into the fundamentals, as well as at some technical analysis. In fact, I do not know too many people trading who go on technical analysis alone; it is just too unnecessarily risky to turn your back on the fundamentals. Instead, I like to take a more comprehensive approach to looking at a stock and keep an eye on the fundamentals—and on what I am hearing from others about it. I guess small investors sitting at their computers do not really have access to the thoughts of other traders, but they can make due. I would not suggest going to chat rooms at all, however; they are the blind leading the blind in the best cases. In the worst cases, you go to a chat room and someone in there is pumping a stock, so enough naive people buy into it, and he or she takes their money. This sort of place is not where one should go to confirm a pattern completion at all. The fundamentals are a lot of help if they come in with something concrete, but we almost never have the luxury of things being that clear. Then you turn to your rules regarding whether a reversal has occurred.

I guess that depends a lot on the stock, as well as on the window that a trader is looking to invest in. If you are saving for retirement or something long term of that sort, and your money is sitting in some blue chip that went down 3 points, this is hardly the time for panic and scrutinizing of the marketplace. If you are a day trader, however, you could have just lost a lot of money on the 3-point decline and may be thinking about what you can get for your furniture at that point. Especially the people trading on margin, they can take a bath with some minor movements. I like to let a stock stay on the opposite side of a trend for some time and also make sure that it is getting away from the trend. And sure, I lose out on the initial part of the reversal, but if the reversal is so small and short-lived that I cannot even take time to confirm it or I lose out on the opportunities, then I probably do not want to be in on that anyway.

Q: When you refer to analyzing stocks in an open-minded fashion, what are some things that people can keep in mind that otherwise might be overlooked?

A: Well, beyond what I have already mentioned, such as the fundamentals, people should try to picture the market as a whole and how the stocks they are trading fit into the fray. For example, in my opinion, it is not the best strategy to look at all stocks the same way; some stocks clearly are better than others or get special treatment from the markets. A lot of it has to do with real reasons for the market to be justified in reacting differently to one stock or another. Size is a good example. A small stock is not the same as a big stock on the market. I think volume is very important for smaller stocks, whereas for larger stocks, by the time volume gets so big that it becomes an anomaly, it is evident that a big stock is on the move. What I mean by this is that a small stock need not be traded very frequently, but when it is, the changes will be significant. Hence the technical indicators that one would look at for that stock should be selected accordingly. One should definitely keep an eye on the volume patterns of a smaller stock, since it will be more responsive. A larger stock, and especially a more widely held stock, should not be as responsive and agile in turbulent market conditions. A big change should take longer, because accumulation and distribution patterns have to be more drawn out because of the sheer size of the trading that must occur. Hence momentum should be a more reliable indicator for these bigger stocks.

Q: What sort of trading strategy should a small investor be planning?

A: This is an important question because one cannot understate the importance of having a plan and sticking to it. An investor who has not sat down and drawn up a plan on paper, or on a computer, is just guessing, stabbing in the dark. The idea behind a plan is to think about what it is that the investor wants to do with his or her money and then where is the best place to go with it. This is the basic idea behind financial planning on a personal level. If people do not have this under their belts, they really have no business moving to the next level, which is portfolio building and technical analysis. Once an individual decides what to do with his or her money, he or she goes and invests some portion in the stock markets, according to risks or whatever his or her criteria are. The individual at this stage has to decide what it is he or she wants to buy. It is at these points that this person should think about what kind of a portfolio he or she wants and what his or her objective is.

Often in this scenario an individual will draw up a portfolio, analyze stocks, and chose those which are best suited for his or her needs. Loosely speaking, we can say that the individual has created some sort of an investment plan, although everyone will have a different format, and some people's plans will be more detailed than others. What often happens after this is that individuals fall into the trap of abandoning their plans due to the developments that occur in the markets on a day-to-day basis. This is problematic because if someone sets out to plan an investment strategy, with clearly defined portfolio objectives, buys stocks that are supposedly the kinds of stocks that can accomplish the investment goals of the individual and so on, this sort of planning should not be tossed aside on a whim. And yet many people turn their backs on all their work and abandon their investment goals or do not follow their plan all the way through to completion and fail to achieve their objectives. Afterward, they think that they were not smart enough as investors or that they did not have the skills. The fact is that they did have the necessary skills, because it really does not take that much, so long as one keeps modest and reasonable goals. What these individuals are lacking is the patience to stay the course they set out for themselves.

Q: We have seen technical analysis used for individual stocks, but many people like to buy mutual funds. What are your thoughts on this? Would you agree that technical analysis is applicable to mutual funds?

A: Well, technical analysis certainly can be used to analyze mutual funds; I would agree with you there. I think that people should understand just what a mutual fund is. It is just a portfolio of stocks chosen on the basis of some stipulated criterion. For example, a tech fund will chose technology stocks, and an index fund will chose a portfolio to match some established market index. Just as you can analyze a portfolio of stocks, and in fact many technicians do so, you can analyze a mutual fund. In fact, the difference between a moving average and a market portfolio is that a moving average tries to eliminate the errors and noise that appear as a by-product of market trading over time, but of one stock. The market portfolio tries to eliminate the errors and noise that appear as a by-product of the same trading, over many stocks, but at the same time. Both are averaging away errors. Hence, if we can use moving averages in technical analysis, we can use mutual funds as well. A caveat is in order here, however. Individuals believe that mutual funds are a panacea of investment security and that they will always do well choosing these because of their bright management. The fact is that while money managers are for the most part exceptional traders, they are also working under tremendous burdens brought on by the sheer size of their portfolios, and the competitive nature and scrutiny of their industry sometimes skew how they trade. For this reason, mutual funds sometimes end up doing about as well as an index portfolio. A small investor who tries to beat the market by buying dozens of different mutual funds has made a grave mistake. He or she is averaging away any potential profit opportunities that his or her investments would make. Usually this sort of strategy does worse than the market portfolio. What is worse, this individual will assume all the management costs and capital gains of all these mutual funds, so I would anticipate that his or her return would not be very impressive. Overbuying mutual funds is a big mistake that is very easy to avoid.

Q: We have seen many techniques for looking at a stock. What sorts of analyses would be overlooked by both technical and fundamental analysts working out of their homes?

A: One mistake that people often make is to look at all companies as if they were the same. We have already talked a little bit about the differences between a big and a small stock in terms of company size. Another difference that people overlook in analyzing companies is that not all companies are the same in terms of their internal organization or product development. For example, suppose there are two companies that are identical in size, stock price, past history, and other fundamental and technical indicators. Now suppose that one of them makes doorknobs for houses. The other company makes martini glasses, picture frames, computer monitors, alarm clocks, holds sugar and soy farming concerns in South America, clothing in Asia, has stakes in oil companies, makes shaving cream, jet planes—you get the idea. The second company is not easily pigeonholed into one sector or another. The first company makes a single product. It may be very successful at it, but it depends exclusively on this product. Changes to the demand of this product or the market structure of the sector in which this product is sold, legislative changes regarding this product, changes in the tax code, import or export restrictions—any one of these could be a potentially devastating change for this company. If one of its intermediate products increases in price, anything, the company's weakness is its total lack of diversification. As a result, investors should factor this into the analysis, because you can bet that everyone else on Wall Street is looking at these issues very closely.

Q: What else do people on Wall Street consider to be important that perhaps small investors are overlooking when considering stocks in which to invest?

A: Last month I saw a program on TV that was designed to help small investors get started in this process. The first thing they brought up was mutual funds and the potential gains from last year's winners. I do not know what the producers of this show had in mind, but there is no reason to be touting last year's best stocks or mutual funds in a show. People are likely to invest in these based on the erroneous expectation that this year those same mutual funds will do well. Anyone who believes this sort of strategy is likely to be disappointed. I think this is a potential mistake that a small investor could make, in that the markets may strike small investors as broad, with many diverse companies and mutual funds in which to invest. In this situation, one naturally looks for some filtering process, some way to sort out the winners from the losers. Picking last year's winners is not the way to go. The markets are not a popularity contest; they are based on returns, and this is what the small investor should be looking for. Additionally, some people like to add their two cents into where small investors have a real buying opportunity. This is especially the case in the sorts of television programs that I am referring to here. They are quite misleading for investors, because individuals touting one stock or another most likely have a vested interest in moving the stock price in some direction that is favorable to their or someone else's position. For example, if a commentator on some program or some guest says that some company that no one has heard of is suddenly a good buy opportunity, it is natural to think that this individual has a long position in the stock and is attempting to boost its price. Even if the individual has no position in the stock per se, just the fact that he or she is saying on television that this stock is now a good buy opportunity creates a situation in which this individual can profit. No one but these individuals know ahead of time what they will say. As a result, they can make money based solely on the fact that they have an opportunity to voice opinions on stocks. These are two mistakes that people often make. They are picking stocks or mutual funds solely for the reason that they have done well in the past, and they are picking stocks or mutual funds because someone on TV happened to mentioned that they presented a profit opportunity.

Q: What applications of technical analysis have you found most helpful in looking at a stock?

A: I like the moving averages, and sometimes the momentum indicators are also a good signal. I like these because they make a lot of sense in terms of what they are picking up in the stock, and they are not quite so ad hoc as to the reasons why they should work. That is, we do not have to take it on faith that they present valid information about the future movements of stock prices; we can understand mathematically what it is that these highlight and then judge if the information that they bring to the forefront is worthwhile to consider based on its own merit and not because someone somewhere said it worked once for them. I find all these sorts of technical indicators to be helpful in terms of understanding the market conditions and what the price has done in the past. It is crucial for understanding where the market is now and what it might be doing, but I do not believe that these indicators can be used to pinpoint turns in the trends, let alone where the price will go once it has turned. I know that there are many technicians who concede these as limitations and work within the constraints of not knowing these things, and their approach makes a lot of sense to me. I do not know anyone who looks at a chart and pretends to know where the market tops and market bottoms are. It is unwise, in my opinion, to believe that you can pick out where the market will turn when it has reached its high and its low. Using technical indicators of any sort with this sort of rigid and literal interpretation would be an abuse of what even the staunchest supporters of technical analysis had intended. Instead, perhaps a better approach would be for an investor to pick out a price range where he or she believes that the price is increasing and buy, not worrying about catching the price at the market bottom. The truth is that no one really knows where market bottoms are.

Q: What about when an investor is already in a stock and is watching the charts and the data to decide if the stock will turn against him or her. What do you suggest here?

A: Well, if an investor is holding a stock, I am assuming that small investors do not normally short stocks, at least in the beginning. Later on, I am sure some do, but most people who have spoken to me look to buy, not to sell short. Some do not even know this option exists. Anyway, if we are assuming that the person is holding a long position, the individual should keep in mind his or her investment objectives, and let it ride. Usually people think that if the stock is going up, they can pick out where the top of the market is. This is nonsense. It is better to sit on it and watch it go up. If it falls back some, then so be it. Like I said before, selling at market tops is a difficult, if not impossible, task. Small investors should be trying to win the war, not the battle. If you are constantly looking to get out when the market falls back a small amount, you are going to take it from the commissions that you pay to get in and out of the stock. Letting profits ride is important for small investors. Equally important, however, is cutting losses. I know, this sounds completely contradictory given what I just said. This is the big question in the market game. What is the difference between cutting your losses early and erroneously getting out of a stock that is whipsawing on its way upward? The answer is usually hindsight. The problem as I see it is in the details. You do not want to pull out of a stock that has fallen back 2 points if you are a medium- to long-term investor. This loss represents less than the round-trip commissions that you will have to pay to get out and back into the stock. You may lose profits doing so as well if it goes higher by the time you get back in. The problem of not cutting losses lies in that people sit on a total dog stock waiting for this thing to rebound. They have lost money on it already and just will not give up on it. Day traders are especially sensitive to this situation and almost unanimously agree that sitting on these sorts of situations is a mistake. If a stock is headed down that road, get out as early as possible, and just get over the loss. It is better to cut a loss early than to sit on it, let profitable opportunities pass one by, and take the same loss further down the road. This situation has additional implications for investors, because a stock that is down will stay down and a stock that is up will stay up. Hence, waiting for this thing to come back can be a losing proposition from all sides.

Q: Thank you for your comments. Any last words of advice?

A: You're welcome. Yes, I would suggest to people that they should be optimistic and patient when regarding their skills as investors. I think anyone can do this, and besides, it is only money. If you decide you are no good at this, rest assured that it is not the most important thing.

Q: Can an ordinary investor realistically expect to make money in the markets, where all the heavy-hitting investment banks and traders are trading?

A: Why not? Sure. Let's think about it in the most simple terms. We always hear people repeating the statement that the stock market historically shows a long-term increasing trend. Think about it. Since the 1960s, the stock market has, on average, given a 9 to 10 percent annual rate of return. Thus, unless one is making stupid decisions over and over again, there is no reason why one cannot make money in the market. All that one needs is some patience and a decent sense of judgment, and one will get a decent return in today's market. And the stock market is like an ever-increasing pie. It is not like your gain is my loss. So who really cares what the heavy hitters are doing? They can make their billions while the ordinary investor can make his or her thousands.

Now if you are looking to make a killing in the market, like to always do better than the market average, then you might not be that successful right off the bat. Say, if you start day trading, it would take time for the payoffs to roll in. Actually, I think most people would tell you that if you start off as a day trader and you do not lose money, you are really lucky. But after you have put in your time, say, a few months or so, you should be fine.

Technological advances really have made investing easy and widely accessible. You can log onto the Internet while fishing in the Florida Everglades to check your stock quotes and charts. It is not like 20 years back when you would have to wait a day to open up the newspaper or turn on the TV and then get only partial news. If anything, the ordinary investor has never had a fairer shot at making money in the market than he or she does today.

Q: With a small amount of investment capital, what trading method should a small investor choose?

A: I think one should start by playing the game safe and gradually learn the tricks of the market before going into riskier trades. Small investors have less money to play with, and if they are rash, they are out of the market before you can say, "I love to day trade." It is probably better for the small investor to go for stocks we have all heard of and stocks one can easily get information about instead of jumping in and buying stuff like penny stocks. Again, it is really easy to get information about stocks on the Internet or from magazines. The Internet is probably a better source of information because it gets updated so often, and it does not cost anything. I am not talking about high-level information here. Just information as to how the market is moving and what the general news is. One can trade and make a decent amount by following such procedures.

It is important that investors develop a trading strategy that they are comfortable with and that they learn to discipline themselves. Discipline is the key. The world around you may change, with people doing all sorts of strange things, but you must stick to your game plan. To last in the market, one must learn to take hits. As soon as you take hits, you should not just quit. You should learn from the experience and move on.

Q: Should the beginner go it alone or go to an investment professional?

A: You are asking me that? Oh, of course, anyone with any time on his or her hands should go it alone. Anyone, trust me, anyone, can get a reasonable sense of the market pretty quickly. The market has its risks and rewards. Who can better figure out what combination of risks and rewards suits you than you yourself? So I say spend some time researching the market, and you are better off than going to a professional and paying huge premiums for his or her advice. What you could gain by the supposed superior analysis, you lose in higher payments for those services. Now, if you are really, really busy with your job or do not want to deal with any stress, then go to a professional or a mutual fund and be happy with the 5 percent or so it offers every year. But think about it. How risky can the market be as long as you are not too greedy? As an investor friend of mine put it, "What's the tension for? Just buy Microsoft stocks and you are set."

Q: How would a beginner ever catch up with a person who has been in the market for a long time?

A: It is difficult. The beginner must learn faster. But the fact is that—and you will be impressed because I will sound mathematically sound here—the returns to learning in the stock market are exponential at initial stages of learning, but the returns decline. So is the difference between a novice and a person who has been in the market for 10 years is greater than the difference between a person who has been in the market for 1 year and a person who has been in the market for 11 years. The longer one is in the market, the less pronounced such differences are. Anyway, I do not think we should discuss this issue more because it really does not matter.

Q: How did you start off in the market? What sort of strategies did you follow?

A: I started off with some money my mother left me as a gift. I was in school and needed a source of income. I decided to put that money to use in the market. I quickly got sucked into trading. The 1990s were an easy time to be making money because the market was doing so well. I got a taste of easy money, although I was a bit too cautious of an investor. Luckily for me, I did jump on the technology stock bandwagon. I, however, managed to stay away from the biotechnology stocks because their fate was so closely tied to Food and Drug Administration authorization. And on reflection I consider myself extremely fortunate that I did not get carried away by the Internet stock hype.

My timings in the market were never anywhere near perfect when I began (they still are not perfect, but I am better now). I would very often leave the market too soon or buy in too late. Sometimes I would sell off my stocks thinking that the prices must have topped off, but I would wait to see that the price actually had risen even further. Many times I missed the opportunity to buy at the lowest price. But despite losing out on some profit opportunities, I was not exactly hurting. I got braver with time and started spending more and more time following my stocks. Pretty soon I became very interested in day trading, and today I am a day trader. I was particularly fascinated by the fact that by trading in real time I could profit from trading stocks with very tight bid-ask spreads.

Q: What sorts of backgrounds do day traders come from?

A: You will be surprised. There are people from all sorts of backgrounds. Starting from bold young investors who want their share of the pie to housewives wanting to make money sitting in their homes. A lot of those who join are really motivated. They are risk takers who are interested in trying out something new and that has the promise of being a more efficient system. Then there are those who entered because they thought it would be "cool" to trade online and not have to go through brokerage houses but who actually did not have a sense of what direct access trading actually entailed. These groups of individuals are likely to suffer heavy losses in the market. They are the ones who give day trading a bad name.

Q: How does one approach the issue of estimating future stock prices? Can one do so reasonably? I mean, is there any point trying?

A: You make it sound like a really hard question. I do not really look at complex mathematics for this. I guess for me it comes instinctively. Do not get me wrong. There are times I have been dead wrong, but usually I can sense market moves. I use a combination of technical and fundamental tools. I follow around 20 or so stocks in the market very closely and see what their fundamentals are as well as look at price and volume charts to see what I think might happen. When I use both together, I am more often right than wrong. You see, while technical tools can give you a sense of where the price is heading in general, they cannot really tell you much if there are shocks or surprising news. So you have got to keep up with the market news, news of a company, and all that. Say the CEO of Coke died in plane crash along with the formula. Coke stock would plummet, right? But technical analysis would not pick this up. I am very careful about new information that comes into the market. I mean, I do not spend as much time on news as a person who follows only the fundamentals because that is also a waste of time. I think that one must know how to maintain a balance between how much time one has and how much information one would like to process. If you have too much information, you just waste time thinking about what to do with it and keep getting more confused and indecisive. If you have been in the market long enough and you have seen the good times and the bad times and you have a sense of how the price moves, you know how to use your judgment.

There are economists who do all sorts of funky maths and statistics to forecast the future movements of prices. All these are frankly beyond me. I do get some consolation from the fact that these people are wrong as often as they are right. So much for their high-tech analysis. But I should not really be putting them down because it really is hard to predict the future, and while it is hard enough to predict tomorrow, it is far harder to predict what will happen a month or a year from now.

Q: You were speaking of information and how you found too much of it counterproductive. What do you mean by this? How would you judge what is good information from bad?

A: Yes, I do think too much information gets in the way of using one's judgment. Information is crucial to success, but there is some optimal level of it. After that level, information just does not add much value. The way to judge good information is certainly from its source. Say the information provided in the reports of the huge investment corporations is very valuable indeed, and this is why one must pay a high amount to have it. Information on free sources is less valuable, but some of the sources are very reliable. Think about Yahoo!'s financial service or something like CNNFN. All the information these sources provide is good to know, although perhaps it is a bit useless for the purpose of profit making because these sources are in the public domain. But while you may not make profits using the information, you will surely lose money if you are unaware of the developments described. What I find very unreliable is Internet chat groups. I think the chats are just pointless blabbering, and a lot of the discussion there is based on discussions generated by rumor mongers. I mean, think about it. Why would anyone want to share information that is worth anything for free and also with people they do not even know? I think users of chat groups are either naïve if they think they are profiting from it, or they simply have a lot of time on their hands to waste.

Q: Honestly tell me what do you think of day trading? Is it for the regular middle-of-the-road investor? What are its risks? Every now and then we read of people losing money in day trading . . .

A: I think day trading is not an enterprise for the faint hearted. One has to be willing to take huge financial hits at times, and the emotional costs of this are very high for many people. Also, it is time-consuming. One has to be attentive to market movements and act sharply on such movements. However, for individuals who love following the marketplace and have the time and energy to dedicate themselves to day trading, I think day trading can be awesome. Having access to real-time data and being able to execute trades instantaneously—it is a good bargain. Unfortunately, there is no secret to success here. You cannot just follow a couple of technical indicators and expect to be making money. The market is always changing, and you must take this into account while choosing which technical indicator to use. For example, in a market that is sharply fluctuating, you probably want to use a moving-average line of relatively shorter duration to get a better idea of the market. This is so because the prices are changing so fast that an average that is over a longer duration would suppress more vital information.

Q: We often hear the statement that a true day trader is not an investor and should not become an investor. What is your take on this?

A: I kind of agree with that. I mean, I think you should have dual lives if you are a day trader. Set aside money so that you can invest in stocks that you like for the long term. And keep the accounts for day trading separate. It is ideal if you can discipline yourself to do this. It is hard, though. I told you about how you must have discipline for day trading. If you make a rule, you must stick to it. The way you profit from day trading is by trading frequently. You cannot have two sets of principles for two sets of stocks that you have set aside for day trading. Do not misunderstand. You can have different strategies for different stocks based on what they are doing, but the principle you apply to them is that if they are in the same situation, you will follow the same strategy. You cannot follow this principle if you are juggling between a buy and hold strategy and a day trading strategy.

You see, many times inexperienced investors start day trading because they think it is the latest fad. They do not quite know how much hard work it involves. They start getting confused and frustrated when things do not go their way. Often the market plays games with individuals, and they give into it. Say you are convinced that a stock will rise in value and you are following a buy and hold policy. You are waiting for it to rise any moment now, and it does not. However, you do not sell it, and you move on to something else because your gut tells you that the price will rise as soon as you sell it and then you'll regret having sold it. So you let the stock just sit in your account. As this wait-and-see period gets longer, you get more frustrated while a world of opportunities is passing your way and you are avoiding them. Sooner or later you will give in. One fine day you see the price down because there is some bad news, and you sell it. But it was the wrong time to sell. The price actually begins to climb after you decided to sell, and you feel like a complete idiot, cursing your luck. All this would not have happened if you were a more agile trader.

Q: There is often confusion in the minds of people as to the difference between online brokerage firms and day trading firms. I mention day trading to people and they often say, "Oh yeah, E*TRADE and all that." What is the difference between the two?

A: There is a big difference between an online brokerage firm and a day trading firm. People really do not know the advantages of day trading firms. If you place orders at online brokers, they are not carried out straightaway. But through day trading you have direct access to the Nasdaq and the New York Stock Exchange (NYSE). You do not have to deal with any intermediaries, but you are directly connected with other traders and market makers, and you get first-hand knowledge of the market conditions. By being able to trade directly, you save a lot of time, and you can trade in real time. The whole process is just very smooth and quick. You do not have to go through a dreaded middleman like the broker who does not have your interest always at the top his or her mind. Instant access to the market minimizes your trading risk and gives you the option to quickly exit a bear market. But you see more than anything it gives you a sense that you are a truly independent investor and that you are the shaper of your destiny.

Q: What sort of software program or system should a day trader choose? Are they usually difficult to use?

A: No, not difficult to use at all. Anyone can use them. As far as the software package, of course, one must go for the one that executes orders the fastest. But not only that. You want the system to be reliable and relatively cheap compared with what else is around. You must weigh all these things. Say a slightly more expensive service may just be much faster and more reliable. Then you would be penny wise and pound foolish if you relied on the cheaper service. I do not want to mention any packages by name here because I do not believe in promoting things I am not paid for (laughter).

Q: Ok, now back to technical questions. If you see a price pattern and you believe that it has completed, when do you jump in and buy on the buy signal and when do you sit and wait to see if the reversal is genuine? Do you base your decision on a price movement of a certain size or on a certain amount of time on the opposite side of the trend line?

A: I would first make sure that the trend is in fact turning. Remember the Dow principle you mentioned in this book, that trends are assumed to continue until there is a definite signal that they are clearly over. Thus I would look at a couple of other technical indicators to see if they indicate that the price pattern is actually likely to be complete. If I am sure that the price will turn, I wait for the earliest opportunity to act. Timing can never be precise in this, but you do not need to be absolutely precise also.

Like any other good technician, I always try to see volume to judge price movements. I also always look at the market to see if there is any change in the overall market or in the particular company fundamentals. Thus I look at a host of indices. I think I look at both the size of price movement and its duration. For instance, say price has been hovering about the same level for a while and is constantly failing to move up. If this situation is accompanied by light trading volume, my guess would be that the price will turn downward, and I would decide to sell. In this case, although the price has not changed much, the duration of its remaining relatively still is a clue to me that price will in fact fall.

Q: Do you find yourself using more of technical or fundamental analysis while looking to pick stocks to trade?

A: As I mentioned earlier, even for day trading purposes, technical analysis on its own would be an inadequate tool. At least, this is my experience. Thus I do both. I look at technical tools to see price movements, whereas the fundamentals provide me with an anchor for doing so. I cannot know the fundamentals of too many stocks out there, but neither can I go through the charts of all stocks. Constrained by my knowledge and my ignorance, I do the best I can. I look at things this way. I see both fundamental and technical forces at work. If they are pointing to the same direction, I am double sure of my strategy. If they do not, I can weigh my options and decide which of the forces is stronger. Alternatively, I often just sit out the period if I cannot reconcile the two forces at all and decide what is likely to happen. Eventually, stock prices clearly gravitate toward their fundamental value. As day traders, we like to take advantage of the interim price adjustment path.

Q: How much analysis goes into each of your stock picks?

A: Well I think quite a bit—especially for stocks that make up huge portions of my portfolio. I like to analyze their fundamentals well, and I look at the technical indicators to see if there is enough action surrounding the stock. There is no point in my buying a stock if its price will remain stable over the next few weeks or months. I am then losing out on other profitable opportunities. Thus I like stocks with a healthy level of action surrounding them.

In addition to the stocks that I decide on carefully, there are also the stocks that I buy because perhaps I heard someone in passing put in a good word. Or maybe I heard an analyst speak highly of it at CNNFN. These stocks I invest in more on a trial-and-error basis. If they work out, I invest more in them, and if they do not, I simply drop them. I do not really lose much because they are relatively minor portions of my portfolio anyway. I am always on the lookout for stocks that are actively trading in the market and are showing quite a bit of variation in prices.

Q: Do you mean the more volatile a stock, the greater your interest in it?

A: You put me in a difficult position. There definitely is an upper limit to volatility that I find acceptable. But let me tell you that I love volatility, and a stock must be really volatile for me to get turned off by it. You know that volatility of stock prices is what makes the day trader tick. Since he or she can exit or enter the market so quickly, he or she can be in or out of the market almost instantly. Thus, if he or she is alert, his or her losses would be limited, but on the upside, his or her profits could be very high. This is what modern technology has made possible.

I know one thing—that a stock with no volatility does not interest me in the least. How do I profit from a price that does not move much? I might as well keep my money in an interest-free checking account as in a stock with no variation. However, if I already own a stock and it suddenly loses its volatility, say, it moves sideways because it is unable to make up its mind as to where it wants to eventually end up, I try to be patient. I do not unload it immediately. I hold onto it, and if after a while I see price rising, I sell it once price has risen to a reasonable level. If, on the other hand, I see price moving downward, I am quick to sell it off. One must be swift to act in the market, but one must not be impatient.

Q: Over time, how do you change your market strategy? Do you do so often?

A: All I am in the market for is to get the biggest bang for my buck. For this I constantly monitor my portfolio and update it. But I try to use my judgment in making such decisions instead of letting feelings such as frustration or disappointment with the market affect me. This was very hard for me to achieve, but now I can do it with greater ease. I do not feel that I change my strategy significantly over time. I am more comfortable using the term *updating strategy.*

Q: We have seen many techniques for looking at a stock. What sorts of analysis would be overlooked by both technical and fundamental analysts working out of their homes?

A: This is tough to answer. I would say that fundamental analysis is a rather mechanical index. It values stock prices depending on company financial statements, the growth opportunity of the company, the overall health of the economy, and all that. What is missing here is a sort of personalized analysis. Say some intangible things like worker morale, or the respect the research division of a company gets may affect the long-run performance of a company. If the work atmosphere is good, the company will be more productive, whereas if the research group is looked at with respect, the brighter brains will probably stick out coming up with new products. While technical analysis claims to be based on human emotions, it does not quite suggest that we chart future price paths depending on psychological factors like worker morale.

In general, it is important to have a sense of the general mood in the market. While many would argue that this is why we look at the price, since price has everything we need to know about the market, I still think it is always a good idea to look at other things. Investor sentiment may not be reflected immediately in the price, and it is a good idea to know how others are thinking or feeling.

Q: What applications of technical analysis have you found most helpful in looking at a stock?

A: I like to look at the figures concerning volume of trade. This really is the clincher for me. When I look at the levels of volume in the market alongside the price, the market just starts making so much more sense to me. Not just me, but anyone can say something about the future price movements with a certain degree of success if they have information on volume. Besides, I like looking at the indices that give an indication of market strength.

Q: Do you use the concept of Elliott waves in your analysis of the market?

A: No. Who has the time to read waves? It just seems like it would be so hard to do. I am perfectly happy reading price and volume charts and complementing them with a bit of fundamental analysis.

Q: Do you then ever use the Dow theory concepts?

A: Yes, but not explicitly, because I just look at individual stocks. But I am sure in some way or the other I do put some of those ideas to use. I mean, I know that it is supposed to be the backbone of technical analysis.

Q: What is your take on "hot tips" that investors' magazines provide?

A: I do not get this. If it is so hot, why is someone giving it to you for free? Also, now that everyone knows it is hot, it can no longer remain hot. People must have bought and sold it to adjust for its hotness. I think one could skim through magazines or Web sites to see what the buzz around the market is, but not necessarily act on it.

Q: What sort of stocks should a small investor be looking at for long-term holdings?

A: Definitely not Internet stocks (laughter). No, but seriously, for long-term holding purposes, your best bet is to look at fundamentals of stocks and buy stocks that are undervalued and sell stocks that are overvalued. Looking at a stock's fundamentals means looking at many variables. You do not need to worry about technical analysis. Why would you look at technical variables if you do not want to trade frequently? Another thing while selecting stocks is that every individual has different risk preferences. Some are willing to take on more risk than others. Thus an individual must decide what is the best risk and reward tradeoff for him or her.

Q: How would the ordinary investor incorporate wide information and statistics on the aggregate economy?

A: Information on the aggregate economy is very important to keep track of. Say the unemployment rate declines for a third straight quarter and reaches a level of 3.6 percent. The economy would show signs of heating up. The Fed might then put the breaks on the economy by raising interest rates. This is likely to send the stock market plunging. The individual investor can get a sense of the effects of the interest rate hike on his or her stock holdings given how the aggregate market reacted. Not only that. Suddenly a whole string of things would become more expensive for him or her. For example, the mortgage payment on his or her house would be up. Given the impact of the aggregate economy on one's economic well-being, it is unlikely that individuals do not react to what is happening to it.

Q: Thank you for your comments. Any parting words of advice?

A: Oh, thank you. Advice—just do your homework, play hard, and enjoy the game. And to the pessimists, I say, remember that it is better to have invested and lost than to have gained 20 pounds.

GLOSSARY

Accumulation   A sideways market at the bottom of the cycle where Wall Street insiders and the smart money are accumulating stock in anticipation of an impending rally.

Advance-decline (A/D) line   The daily sum of the total number of stocks that went up in price less the total number of stocks that went down in price. The A/D line should move with the market to confirm its direction. If it diverges, the market is thought to be on the verge of a reversal.

All or none   An order to purchase or sell a security in which the broker/ dealer is instructed to fill the entire order or not to fill it at all.

Analyst   An individual employed by large brokerage firms who analyzes the fundamentals of a company and issues earnings expectations and other information relating to the company's stock.

Arbitrage   A transaction in which, given that the same security is selling at two different prices, a security is bought at the lower price and resold at the higher price.

Ask price   The price at which market participants offer to sell a security.

Auction market   A market such as the New York Stock Exchange, where trading occurs in one place and a specialist makes markets and provides liquidity.

Bar chart   A chart that shows the high and low prices of the day for a stock as a long stick or bar. The horizontal peg attached to the side of the bar indicates the closing price.

Basis point   A measure of interest rates, where one basis point is $\frac{1}{100}$ of 1 percent.

Bear   A trader who expects market prices to decline. A trader can also be described as *bearish*.

Bear market   A market with declining prices.

Bid price   The price at which market participants offer to buy a security.

Bond   An investment instrument in which the seller of the bond agrees to pay back the price of the bond as well as a premium.

Bollinger bands   Lines drawn above and below a primary trend line that indicate a confidence region within which price should stay. The distance between a Bollinger band and the estimated primary trend line is calculated on the basis of the estimated standard deviations of the stock price.

Breakout   When price moves above the resistance level or below the support level. A good sign for a breakout is that there is heavy volume accompanying it.

Broker   A financial intermediary who brings buyers and sellers together and charges commissions.

Bull   A trader who expects market prices to increase.

Bull market   A market with increasing prices.

Calendar effects   These are effects relating to the time of year, quarter, month, or even day. For example, it is a stylized fact that stocks seem to do better in January. Also known as *seasonal effects*.

Cheap talk   A term that refers to the ability to send out signals costlessly; e.g., a threat to veto a bill by the President is considered cheap talk.

Commission The charge that a broker collects for serving as the intermediary in a financial transaction.

Consolidation pattern See *Continuation pattern.*

Continuation pattern This is a pattern that forms as a sideways market in the middle of a rally or a decline. The stock has stopped to catch its breath, so to speak. Also known as *consolidation pattern.*

Correction A term referring to a fall in the market of less than 20 percent.

Coupon The interest that is paid to a bondholder for a bond.

Day order An order that is specified to be filled within the day it is placed or else canceled.

Day trader A trader who closes out all positions at the end of the day for cash.

Dealer-driven market A market, such as the Nasdaq, where multiple market makers compete against each other as providers of liquidity.

Distribution A pattern that forms as a rectangle at market tops where Wall Street insiders and informed investors are said to be distributing stock to uninformed investors in anticipation of an impending fall in the stock price.

Downbid A decrease of one level in the price of a stock on the Nasdaq.

Downtick A decrease in the price of a stock on the New York Stock Exchange of one level, in which a trade has taken place.

Electronic Communication Networks (ECNs) The virtual markets where Nasdaq stocks trade.

Envelopes Lines that are drawn parallel to an estimated trend line at some fixed distance from the stock price. These lines often are used as indicators that the stock is making a large move if the price wanders past one of them. See also *Bollinger bands.*

Equity Ownership in a firm, e.g., by ownership of stock issued by a firm.

Fundamental analysis Analyzing the potential changes in the price of a stock based on the company's fundamentals, such as the P/E ratio, debt ratio, and so on.

Fundamentals Information relating to a company that is used to predict the success and profitability of the company by some market participants. Some fundamentals may be debt ratio, market share, etc.

Gap When a stock price opens at a different price than it closed the previous day.

Good-till-canceled An order with a restriction that stipulates that the order is in effect until canceled.

Index fund A mutual fund whose basket of stocks is the same as the basket used by some market index of securities.

Institutional investor A term used to refer to firms that invest in the stock market, instead of individuals.

Inside market The best prices available for trading, the highest bid and the lowest ask.

Leverage A term referring to debt, often used to describe how much of an investment or position is financed by borrowing.

Limit order An order to be filled only at a price no worse than a specified price level, called the *limit price.*

Liquidity The ability to enter/exit an investment or make a transaction quickly and at low costs because there are buyers and sellers willing to take opposite position.

Listed stocks Stocks sold on the New York Stock Exchange.

Long position When an investor owns a stock in anticipation of a price increase. Selling stock that one owns is called a *long sale.*

Marker maker A market participant responsible for providing liquidity, i.e., who stands ready to buy or sell from traders.

Market order An order to be filled immediately as it is placed and at the current market prices.

Market risk The risk that the value of any one stock will be affected by the general value of other assets on the market.

Money market The market for securities with short-term maturity, usually less than 1 year.

Mutual fund A company that invests the aggregate money of its shareholders in the markets.

NASD National Association of Securities Dealers. The organization whose member firms make markets in the Nasdaq markets.

NYSE New York Stock Exchange.

Offer The price at which a market maker offers to sell a stock.

Open outcry   The system of trading stocks in which individuals gather around a prespecified trading area and shout out the bids and offers.

Order flow   A term referring to the stream of buying amounts that are observed by, for example, a specialist on the New York Stock Exchange. Another example would be large brokerage firms who observe internal order flow from their clients.

Over-the-counter   A market for securities in which trading occurs off an organized exchange, among brokers and investors.

Penetration   When the price moves beyond a resistance or support line or some other boundary implied by technical analysis as having the effect of signaling a potential change in the underlying primary trend. See also *Breakout*.

Primary market   The market for securities when they are offered initially to the public and have not been traded previously.

Primary trend   The trend that is said to be governing the general movement of a stock price in the long run. This trend captures the general direction of the stock price over long periods of time.

Profit taking   When a sell-off of some stock ensues because investors feel that the price is high and they want cash instead of the stock.

Pure discount bond   A bond such as a Treasury bill that pays no coupon but sells at a discount from its par value.

Quote   The description of the market for a stock, which includes bid and ask prices, as well as the size of the quantities supplied and demanded at those prices.

Rally   When the price of a stock steadily increases.

Rectangle   A pattern of price movement in which the price bounces back and forth from a support to a resistance level, and these support and resistance lines are parallel to each other. Hence the price movement forms a rectangle. Also known as a *sideways market*.

Resistance   A price level that represents a psychological barrier for the market beyond which the price of a stock cannot rise. Often, when a stock reaches the resistance level, investors fear that the price will fall, as it has before, and sell, which causes the price to fall.

Return   The increase in wealth (often measured as a percent) due to investing in some asset.

Reversal   When a trend, especially the primary trend, changes direction and the stock moves the other way.

Risk-free rate   The return of an asset with no risk.

Risk premium   The return above the risk-free rate that investors demand for assuming some asset risk.

Scalper   A trader who derives profits from holding assets just long enough to exploit arbitrage opportunities that arise from small price changes.

Secondary market   The market for assets that were issued previously and trade among investors.

Secondary trend   Short-term fluctuations in price that wrap themselves around the primary trend. These are movements in price that have no consequence for the long-term position of the price.

Sell-off   When a large number of shares are offered in the market for a stock, causing its price to fall.

Short position   When an investor sells a stock short.

Short sale   A sale of an asset that is borrowed from a broker and later purchased from the market and returned to the broker. The idea of a short sale is to borrow stock to sell while the price is high and later buy it back to replace the borrowed stock when the price is low.

SOES   Small Order Execution System.

Specialist   The individual who is in charge of making markets and providing liquidity for stocks traded on the New York Stock Exchange.

Spread   The difference between the bid price and the ask price.

Stock index   A measure of the performance of a stock market or some sector of the stock market consisting of an averaging of some or all the stocks traded in the market or sector.

Stop order   An order that calls for the transaction to be filled until the stock price reaches the stop price.

Support   A price level that represents a psychological barrier for the market beyond which the price of a stock cannot fall. Often, when a stock reaches the support level, investors assume that the price will increase, as it has before, and buy, which causes the price to increase.

Technical analysis   Analyzing the behavior of stock price movements over time by way of stock price charts and graphs.

Upbid An increase in the price of a stock on the Nasdaq of one level.

Uptick An increase in the price of a stock on the New York Stock Exchange of one level, in which a trade has taken place.

Whipsaw A temporary change in direction of the price when it is following a general trend. A whipsaw occurs when the price of a stock crosses over a moving-average line, for example, and then crosses back later on and continues its previous trend.

Yield The discount rate for a bond, which equates the present value of the coupons paid by the bond and the principal to the price.

Zero-plus tick When a trade takes place on the New York Stock Exchange for some stock in which price has not changed, but in the previous change, price had increased.

INDEX

ABOUT THE AUTHORS

Rafael Romeu teaches economics and banking at the University of Maryland. In addition to his research on global equity and foreign exchange markets, Romeu is an experienced manager of private sector pension funds. He is the author of *Understanding Direct Access Trading*.

Umar Serajuddin is a graduate of Middlebury College, with a Masters degree from the University of Maryland. He is completing his Ph.D. from The University of Texas. Umar has worked in micro-lending and other financial matters at Grameen Bank and is an avid researcher of the financial markets.